the Playwright

Coward
the Playwright

by

JOHN LAHR

METHUEN . LONDON

To ANTHEA and CHRISTOPHER – Pilgrim Souls

First published in Great Britain in 1982 in simultaneous hardback and paperback editions by Methuen London Ltd, 11 New Fetter Lane, London EC4P 4EE

ISBN 0 413 46840 2
ISBN 0 413 48050 X

Printed and bound in Great Britain by
Butler & Tanner Ltd, Frome and London

The Introduction (Impresario of Himself) has appeared in a slightly different form in *The London Review of Books* (UK) and *Vogue* (USA).
Excerpts from Noël Coward's plays and lyrics as well as passages from his diaries are reprinted by courtesy of the Executors of his Estate. Certain sections of the diaries quoted do not appear in *The Noël Coward Diaries* edited by Graham Payn and Sheridan Morley and published by Weidenfeld and Nicolson in 1982.

Contents

List of Illustrations

(*between pages* 86–87)

1 'Noël the Fortunate: the young playwright, actor, and composer, Mr Noël Coward, busy at breakfast'. From *The Sketch* of 29 April 1925. (Mander and Mitchenson Theatre Collection)

2 Noël Coward as Elyot Chase and Gertrude Lawrence as Amanda Prynne in Act Two of *Private Lives*, Phoenix Theatre, London, 1930. (Photo: Sasha. Reproduced by courtesy of BBC Hulton Picture Library)

3 Noël Coward as Leo, Alfred Lunt as Otto and Lynn Fontanne as Gilda in *Design for Living*, Ethel Barrymore Theatre, New York, 1933. (Mander and Mitchenson Theatre Collection)

4 Gertrude Lawrence and Noël Coward in *Tonight at 8.30*, 24 November 1936. (Cartoon by Frueh)

5 Noël Coward photographed by Cecil Beaton. (Mander and Mitchenson Theatre Collection. Reproduced by courtesy of Sotheby's, Belgravia)

6 Noël Coward in cabaret at Las Vagas. (Photo by William Claxton, Los Angeles. Mander and Mitchenson Theatre Collection)

7 Noël Coward on the stage of the Old Vic Theatre, London, directing *Hay Fever* for the National Theatre, 1964. (Photo: Snowdon)

8 Sir Noël Coward at the Mermaid Theatre, London, at a press conference to launch *Cowardy Custard*, July 1972. (Photo: Douglas H. Jeffery, © 1972)

Frontispiece: Noël Coward caricatured by Hirschfeld. (From *Call Them Irreplaceable* by John Fisher, Elm Tree Books, London, 1976)

Acknowledgements

I am grateful to Nick Hern of Methuen for offering me the opportunity to write this book. Sheridan Morley, Coward's first biographer, also read the manuscript. I appreciate his kindness and magnanimity in letting another critic poach on what is clearly his territory. Raymond Mander and Joe Mitchenson, from whose theatre archive the majority of photographs in this book have been taken, have also provided the Coward fan with an invaluable source book of plots, casts and critical response to the plays: *Theatrical Companion to Coward* (Rockliff, 1957). Richard Avedon has generously contributed his fine portrait of Coward, which appears for the first time in this volume. Joan Hirst, keeper of the Coward scrapbooks and the Coward Estate's business interests, gave me tea and encouragement as I studied the volumes of Coward clippings in her Chelsea flat.

Anthea Lahr, who has a talent to amuse, also has a talent to improve. As in all my books, her editorial skill has been invaluable.

J.L.
London
February, 1982

Noël Coward

1899 Born 16 December. The second of three sons born to Violet and Arthur Coward of Teddington, Middlesex.

1911 Begins professional acting career as Prince Mussel in *The Goldfish*.

1920 *I'll Leave It To You* (1919) produced.

1922 *The Young Idea* (1921) produced.

1923 Plays Sholto Brent in *The Young Idea* in the West End. Appears in the revue *London Calling!* for which he wrote songs and sketches.

1924 *The Vortex* (1923) produced. Coward plays Nicky Lancaster. As playwright and actor, Coward becomes a sensation.

1925 *Hay Fever* (1924), *Easy Virtue* (1924) produced.

1927 Composes 'A Room with a View', 'What's Going to Happen to the Tots'. *Easy Virtue* and *The Vortex* filmed.

1929 Coward writes book, music and lyrics, directs *Bitter-Sweet*. Cecil Beaton: 'By the late twenties, ... Noël Coward's influence spread even to the outposts of Rickmansworth and Poona.'

1930 *Private Lives* produced. Coward plays Elyot Chase to Gertrude Lawrence's Amanda Prynne. Writes 'Mad Dogs and Englishmen'.

1931 *Cavalcade* produced. Coward directs, writes book, music, lyrics including 'Twentieth Century Blues'. *Private Lives* filmed.

1932 Coward writes 'Mad About the Boy', 'Children of the Ritz', 'The Party's Over Now' for the revue *Words and Music. Cavalcade* filmed.

1933 *Design for Living* (1932) produced on Broadway. As Leo Mercure, Coward stars with Alfred Lunt and Lynn Fontanne. Writes 'I'll Follow My Secret Heart', 'Don't Put Your Daughter on the Stage Mrs. Worthington'. *Bitter-Sweet* filmed.

1936 *Tonight at 8:30* produced (ten one-act plays, one of them produced for one performance only).

1937 *Present Indicative* (vol. 1 of Coward's autobiography) published. Writes 'Stately Homes of England'.

1938 *Operette* produced.

1939 *Design for Living* produced in England. Writes *This Happy Breed* and *Present Laughter*.

1940 Tours Australia for the Armed Forces.

1941 Tours New Zealand. Writes 'Could You Please Oblige Us With a Bren Gun', 'London Pride', 'Imagine the Duchess's Feelings'. *Blithe Spirit* produced. Writes screenplay for *In Which We Serve*.

1942 *This Happy Breed, Present Laughter* produced. Coward plays Charles Condomine (*Blithe Spirit*), Frank Gibbons (*This Happy Breed*) and Garry Essendine (*Present Laughter*), also Captain Kinross in the film *In Which We Serve*.

1943 Writes 'Don't Let's Be Beastly to the Germans'. *This Happy Breed* filmed.

1944 *Blithe Spirit* filmed. Writes screenplay for *Brief Encounter* (based on *Still Life*, a play from *Tonight at 8:30*).

1946 The musical *Pacific 1860* produced.

1947 *Peace in Our Time* (1946) produced.

1950 The musical *Ace of Clubs* produced.

1951 *Relative Values* (1950) produced.

1952 *Quadrille* produced. Writes 'There Are Bad Times Just Around the Corner'.

1953 Begins career as cabaret entertainer at Café de Paris singing medley of his songs.

1954 *Future Indefinite* (vol. 2 of Coward's autobiography) is published. Writes 'A Bar on the Piccola Marina'. Coward's mother dies on 30 June.

1956 *Nude with Violin* (1954) produced. Coward takes up tax exile in Bermuda.

1959 Shifts base to Les Avants, Switzerland.

1960 *Waiting in the Wings* (1959) produced.

1961 The musical *Sail Away* produced under Coward's direction. Writes *Sunday Times* articles against the English new wave in drama.

1964 *Hay Fever* revived at the National Theatre under Coward's direction.

1966 *Suite in Three Keys* (1965) produced. Coward's last appearance on the West End stage.

1970 Coward knighted.

1972 *Cowardy Custard*, an anthology of Coward songs, produced with great success in London. Another anthology *Oh! Coward*, produced for a Toronto nightclub. After a long tour of North America, the show ends up on Broadway (1973).

1973 Cowards dies on 26 March in Jamaica.

Introduction

IMPRESARIO OF HIMSELF

'Mr. Coward ... is his own invention and contribution to this century ...

John Osborne

Noël Coward never believed he had just a talent to amuse. A man who spent a lifetime merchandising his de-luxe persona, Coward liked to make a distinction between accomplishment and vanity: 'I am bursting with pride, which is why I have absolutely no vanity.'[1] A performer's job is to be sensational; and in his songs, plays and public performances, Coward lived up to the responsibility of making a proper spectacle of himself. His peers had difficulty in fathoming this phenomenon. T. E. Lawrence thought Coward had 'a hasty kind of genius'.[2] Sean O'Casey spat spiders at the mention of his name: 'Mr. Coward hasn't yet even shaken a baby-rattle of life in the face of one watching audience.'[3] J. B. Priestley, as late as 1964, taxed him mischievously: 'What is all this nonsense about being called the Master?'[4] Shaw, who prophesied success for the fledgling playwright in 1921, warned him 'never to fall into a breach of essential good manners'.[5] He didn't.

A star is his own greatest invention. Coward's plays and songs were primarily vehicles to launch his elegant persona on the world. In his clipped, bright, confident style, Coward irresistibly combined reserve and high camp. He became the merry-andrew of moderation, warning mothers to keep their daughters off the stage, confiding, in *Present Laughter* (1942), that sex was 'vastly overrated' and sardonically pleading: 'don't let's be beastly to the Germans'. Coward was a performer who wrote: not a writer who happened to

1

perform. He wrote his svelte, wan good looks into the role of Nicky Lancaster in *The Vortex* (1924): 'He is extremely well-dressed,' explain the stage directions. 'He is tall and pale, with thin nervous hands'. The play made Coward a sensation both as an actor and as a playwright. Coward was his own hero; and the parts he created for himself were, in general, slices of his legendary life. Leo (*Design for Living*), Charles Condomine (*Blithe Spirit*), Hugo Latymer (*A Song at Twilight*) are all smooth, successful writers. Garry Essendine (*Present Laughter*), George Pepper ('Red Peppers' from *Tonight at 8:30*) and Elyot Chase, a man of no apparent metier in *Private Lives* who nonetheless manages a dance and a few songs at the piano, all exploited Coward's theatrical past. Even in the Second World War, when he hoped his writing talent could be put to some serious use, it was Coward's presence that was valued. 'Go out and sing 'Mad Dogs and Englishmen' while the guns are firing – that's your job',[6] Churchill told him. Coward's massive output (sixty produced plays, over three hundred published songs, plus screenplays, volumes of short stories, autobiography and fiction) contributes to his legend. His work was so successful an advertisement for himself that Kenneth Tynan, I think rightly, observed: 'even the youngest of us will know in fifty years' time what we meant by "a very Noël Coward sort of person".'[7]

Like all great entertainers, Coward knew how to exploit his moment. In the thirties Cyril Connolly was complaining that his plays were 'written in the most topical and perishable way imaginable, the cream in them turns sour overnight.'[8] The American critic Alexander Woollcott dubbed Coward 'Destiny's Tot', but he was England's solid-gold jazz-baby who later turned into an international glamour-puss. Coward swung with the times and suavely teased them. 'I am never out of opium dens, cocaine dens, and other evil places. My mind is a mass of corruption,' he told the *Evening Standard* in 1925.[9] Every new-fangled idiom found its way into his dialogue, even if he didn't always fully grasp its

2

meaning: 'You're psychoanalytic neurotics the both of you', complains one of the characters in *Fallen Angels* (1925). *The Vortex* exploited the clash between Victorian and modern mores, the old and the young idea. *Fallen Angels* and *Easy Virtue* (1925) mined the mother-lode of sex, scandal and pseudo-sophistication. *Cavalcade* (1931) and *This Happy Breed* (1942) spoke directly to the political chauvinism of the day. All these plays had great commercial success and the last two were considered serious patriotic statements about England and her fighting spirit. But Coward was not a thinker (at the mere suggestion O'Casey exclaimed 'Mother o'God!'[10]). His genius was for style. When his plays aspired to seriousness, the result was always slick (O'Casey compares the sketchy characters in *Cavalcade* to 'a tiny monogram on a huge bedspread'[11]); and when he wrote himself into the role of ardent heterosexual lover (*Still Life*, which he himself called the 'most mature'[12] of the one-act plays in *Tonight at 8:30*) or ordinary working-class bloke (*This Happy Breed*), the characterisation is wooden. The master of the comic throw-away becomes too loquacious when he gets serious, and his fine words ring false. Only when Coward is frivolous does he become in any sense profound.

Frivolity, as Coward embodied it, was an act of freedom, of disenchantment. He had been among the first popular entertainers to give a shape to his generation's sense of absence. His frivolity celebrates a metaphysical stalemate, calling it quits with meanings and certainties. 'We none of us ever mean *anything*,' says Sorel Bliss amid the put-ons at the Bliss house-party in *Hay Fever* (1925). The homosexual sense of the capriciousness of life is matched by a capricious style. 'I think very few people are completely normal really, deep down in their private lives. It all depends on a combination of circumstances. If all the various cosmic thingummys fuse at the same moment ...': thus Amanda in *Private Lives* (1930). This high-camp style, of which Coward was the theatrical master, worked as a kind of sympathetic magic to dispel both self-hatred and public scorn. 'Has it ever struck you that flippancy might cover a very real embarrassment?' someone asks, again in *Private Lives*. The most gossamer of his good plays, *Private Lives* is adamant on the subject of frivolity.

> ELYOT (*seriously*): You mustn't be serious, my dear one, it's just what they want.
> AMANDA: Who's they?
> ELYOT: All the futile moralists who try to make life unbearable. Laugh at them. Be flippant. Laugh at everything, all their sacred shibboleths. Flippancy brings out the acid in their damned sweetness and light.
> AMANDA: If I laugh at everything, I must laugh at us too.
> ELYOT. Certainly you must. We're figures of fun all right.

In *Design for Living* (1932), the laughter of the *ménage à trois* reunited at the finale ('they groan and weep with laughter; their laughter is still echoing down the walls as the curtain falls') is frivolity's refusal to suffer. Even as she leaves her third husband, aptly named Ernest, Gilda, like Elyot Chase, insists that she is not serious. The battle in Coward's best comedies is not between licence and control but between gravity and high spirits. At least three times in *Private Lives* people shout at Elyot (Coward's role) to be serious. 'I fail to see what humour there is in incessant trivial flippancy', says Victor, sounding like one of Coward's critics. Like James Agate, for instance, who wrote in the *Sunday Times*: 'Mr. Coward is credited with the capacity of turning out these highly-polished pieces of writing in an incredibly short time, and if rumour and the illustrated weeklies are to be believed, he writes his plays in a flowered dressing-gown and before breakfast. But what I want to know is what kind of work he intends to do after breakfast, when he is clothed and in his right mind'.[13] Elyot, Coward's spokesman, lives in the world of appearances, the world of the moment, and he celebrates it: 'Let's be superficial and pity the poor Philosophers. Let's blow trumpets and squeakers, and enjoy the party as much

4

as we can, like very small, quite idiotic school-children. Let's savour the delight of the moment . . .'

Coward's best work follows, more or less, this recipe for chaos. His reputation as a playwright rests on *Hay Fever*, *Private Lives*, *Design for Living*, *Present Laughter*, *Blithe Spirit* (1941) and the brilliant cameo *Hands Across the Sea* (1936). In all these comedies of bad manners, the characters are grown-up adolescents. There is no family life to speak of, no children, no commitment except to pleasure. The characters do no real work; and money, in a time of world depression, hunger marches and war, is taken for granted. Monsters of vanity and selfishness, they appeal to the audience because their frivolity has a kind of stoic dignity. Written fast and in full, confident flow (*Hay Fever* – five days; *Private Lives* – four days; *Present Laughter* and *Blithe Spirit* – six days), Coward's best work has the aggressive edge of his high spirits (even his bookplates show him winking). And when, in the fifties, his plays no longer found favour, he took frivolity's message to the public in person as a cabaret turn, brilliantly mocking his audiences' appetite for anxiety with such impish songs as 'Why must the show go on?' and 'There are bad times just around the corner':

> With a scowl and a frown
> We'll keep our peckers down
> And prepare for depression and doom and dread,
> We're going to *un*pack our troubles from our old kit bag
> And wait until we drop down dead . . .

'It's all a question of masks,' explains Leo in *Design for Living*. 'Brittle, painted masks. We all wear them as a form of protection; modern life forces us to'. But Coward's acute awareness (and insistence) on the performing self comes out of a homosexual world where disguise is crucial for survival.

In *Present Laughter*, Garry Essendine (a successful actor and another Coward star turn) is trapped in his performance. 'I'm always acting – watching myself go by – that's what's so horrible – I see myself all the time, eating, drinking, loving, suffering – sometimes I think I'm going mad.' Essendine is another of Coward's irresistible heterosexual postures: 'Everyone worships me, it's nauseating'. Garry is fantastically successful – and success can be the most effective mask of all. The jokes in the play belie concerns of a different nature. Although elsewhere Coward sang about following his secret heart and being mad about the boy, he didn't push it on stage. His plays tread cautiously around his deeper meanings. The comedies hurry the audience past issues which the dialogue tries tentatively to raise.

Only in *Semi-Monde* (unpublished, 1929) does Coward find a successful metaphor for the sexual complications that lie behind his posturing. *Semi-Monde* is easily the most visually daring of his comedies, and the most intellectually startling. Set in a swank Paris hotel lobby and bar over the years 1924–1926, with dozens of lovers continually making their predatory exits and entrances, *Semi-Monde* is made up of sexually mischievous *tableaux vivants* and gets much nearer the homosexual knuckle than Coward's public image allowed. The play was never produced in Coward's lifetime. In *Semi-Monde* Coward's camp sensibility has a field day. 'My dear – where did you find that?' says Albert to Beverley, meaning his travelling companion, Cyril. 'It's divine'. And when Beverley goes to buy *Vanity Fair* at the newsstand, Albert pipes up: 'Do get *La Vie Parisienne*, it's so defiantly normal.' In this play, where everyone is on the make, there is no need for Coward's statements about role-playing, the transience of relationships, the need to be light-hearted – his usual comic hobby-horses – because here the game is shown in action. 'I'm going to be awfully true to you', says Tanis to her husband Owen on their honeymoon in 1924. 'I've got a tremendous ideal about it'. But by the third act (1926) she is having an affair with a successful writer, Jerome Kennedy. Owen is smitten by Kennedy's daughter, Norma. It is to the writer, as usual, that Coward allows a few closing moments of articulate disgust: 'We're all silly animals', he says, when the affair is finally out in the open, 'gratifying our beastly desires, covering them with a veneer of decency and good behaviour. Lies ... lies ... complete rottenness ...' But Jerome, like the others, can't and won't change. 'There's nothing to be done, you know – nothing at all.' The only thing left is to put on a good show.

Coward's most vivacious playwrighting is about what Preston Sturges liked to call 'Topic A'. Yet his official theatrical line on sex is not to laugh the issues off the stage, but to treat them with distant superiority. As Garry Essendine admits in *Present Laughter*, 'I enjoy it for what it's worth and fully intend to do so for as long as anybody's interested and when the time comes that they're not, I shall be perfectly content to settle down with an apple and a good book.' Coward's wit fights no battles in his plays except to endear him to his public. 'Consider the public' were the first words of advice to the New Wave in 1961. 'Treat it with tact and courtesy. Never fear or despise it ... Never, never, never bore the living hell out of it'. Coward's laughter is always reassuring, which is why it is still commercial.

Coward has an immense reputation for wit, but unlike the rest of the high-camp brotherhood, Wilde, Firbank and Orton, he rarely essays epigrams, or sports directly with ideas in his plays. 'To me', he maintained, 'the essence of good comedy writing is that perfectly ordinary phrases such as "Just fancy!" should, by virtue of their context, achieve greater laughs than the most literate epigrams. Some of the biggest laughs in *Hay Fever* occur on such lines as "Go on", "No there isn't, is there?" and "This haddock's disgusting". There are many other glittering examples of my sophistication in the same vein ...'[14] Such famous Cowardisms as 'Very flat, Norfolk', 'Don't quibble, Sybil', 'Certain women should be struck regularly like gongs' have the delightful silliness of an agile mind which was never as bold on stage as it was in life. 'Dear 338171,' Coward wrote to the shy T. E. Lawrence in the RAF. 'May I call you 338?'[15] Nor are Coward's theatrical put-downs ('AMANDA: Heaven preserve me from nice women. SYBIL: Your reputation will do

7

that') as bitchy as some of the real-life improvisations like 'Keir Dullea, gone tomorrow'.

Where Coward's humour is incomparable is in his chronicling of the strut and swagger of certain society ladies.

> It was in the fresh air
> And we went as we were
> And we stayed as we were
> Which was Hell ...

It was not the situations of English life (except for *Blithe Spirit* his comedies have no substantial plots) but the sound of it, that interested Coward. When, in *Hay Fever*, Simon Bliss admits to his mother that he hasn't washed, Judith says: 'You should darling, really. It's so bad for your skin to leave things about on it.' Coward loves such fluting vagueness and he has left modern theatre a number of cunning pen portraits of this endangered species. In *Hands Across the Sea*, Lady Maureen 'Piggie' Gilpin is faced with the unexpected arrival of the Wadhursts, a colonial couple with whom she once stayed while travelling in the Far East. Her own breathless social whirl makes it impossible for her ever to get to know them:

> PIGGIE: ... (*The telephone rings*) I've got millions of questions I want to ask you, what happened to that darling old native who did a dance with a sword? – (*At telephone.*) Hallo – (*Continuing to everyone in general.*) It was the most exciting thing I've ever seen, all the villagers sat round in torchlight and they beat – (*At telephone.*) Hallo – yes, speaking – (*Continuing*) beat drums and the – (*At telephone*) hallo – darling, I'd no idea you were back – (*to everbody*) and the old man tore himself to shreds in the middle, it was marvellous – ...

In his memorial to Coward, Kenneth Tynan remarked that Coward 'took the fat off English comic dialogue'.[16] Tynan tried to float the notion that the elliptical patter characteristic of Harold Pinter's plays originated in Noël Coward's. In support, he quoted a line out of context from *Shadow Play* (1935): 'Small talk, a lot of small talk, with other thoughts going on behind.' But Coward's characters live nervily on the surface of life, and say pretty much what they mean. The reticence in the comedies comes not from the characters holding back, but from the author. He defends his artifice to the end. 'Equally bigoted,' he wrote in his diatribe against the New Wave, 'is the assumption that reasonably educated people who behave with restraint are necessarily "clipped", "arid", "bloodless" and "unreal".'[17]

Tynan called Coward 'a virtuoso of linguistic nuance'.[18] But it is a disservice to the splendid energy Coward gave to his half-century to put him so elegantly on the literary shelf. His triumph was noisier and, thankfully, more vulgar. He ventilated life with his persona. And it is the frivolity in his plays which has proved timeless. The reason is simple. Frivolity acknowledges the futility of life while adding flavour to it.

1

The Politics of Charm

'There is nothing that gives more reassurance than a mask'
Colette, *My Apprenticeship*

Once, when asked how he would be remembered by future generations, Noël Coward shrewdly replied, 'By my charm'.[1]

Coward imposed as sharp a sense of form on himself as he did on his plays. The symmetry of both was meant to disarm. The words 'charm' and 'enchanting' dominate Coward's vocabulary of praise. Charm is related etymologically to enchantment, the power to cast a spell. There is no doubt about the appeal of Coward's quick wit and laconic sophistication. By 1925, when he was 25, Coward had already become 'the great celebrated glamorous cookie'[2] he dreamed of being.

'The showman in Coward,' Hesketh Pearson wrote in 1923, 'takes the form of charm, plus excessive volubility. He is "charming" to everybody, and as a consequence he has hosts of admirers. Also no one who can entertain folk with an endless stream of persiflage is ever likely to want for company, and Noël's life is almost passed in a prolonged procession through applauding parties.'[3]

'Life is nothing but a game of make believe,' Coward wrote in one of his earliest songs for *London Calling!* (1923). He'd defined all the world as his stage, and invented a persona to dominate it. Coward's performing self sought conquest and confirmation everywhere. Observing the Coward charm at first hand, Peter Quennell was struck by its cunning:

> He was seldom definitely behind the scenes; and to every situation that occurred he gave a strong dramatic turn ... Off the stage, when did Noël act, and when was his private behaviour totally

spontaneous? Given an audience, he seldom entered a room; he almost always made an entry; and I remember another occasion, this time in a house in France where a number of English guests were assembled. Among them was the singer Olga Lynn – 'Oggie' to her large affectionate circle ... She was recovering from a slight stroke; but of this Noël happened to be unaware. He arrived late and, a suitable entry having been made, moved genially around the room, distributing kisses and smiles and bows, until at last he came to Oggie. 'Darling Oggie; and how are you?' he demanded. 'Thank you, Noël; I've been ill you see', she replied in muffled accents and patted her poor flaccid cheek. Noël dramatically threw up his hands. 'Not – a – tiny – *strokey* – Oggie – darling?' he enquired in tones of heartfelt consternation, spacing out the words and lending each a poignant emphasis ...[4]

On stage and off, charm requires constant vigilance. 'I have taken a lot of trouble with my public face,'[5] Coward said. He wanted his public to be enchanted; he wanted not simply triumph but total surrender. 'Lose yourself', Coward said about acting, 'And you lose your audience'.[6] He kept himself and his public under tight control. 'You've got to control the audience', he said of killing the ripples of small laughs to get the wave. 'They've got to do what I tell them'.[7] Charm was the means by which tyrannical wilfulness was transformed into delight.

The name of charm's game is omnipotence. It is a means of manipulating the world while keeping one's individuality well-defended. Coward's charm was a mask of his insecurity and an admission of his high-spirited ambition. He'd learned early that a good offence is the best defence. 'It's important not to let the public have a loophole to lampoon you',[8] he told Cecil Beaton in 1929, one phenomenon to another. Beaton recounted the conversation in his diary:

That, Coward explained, was why he studied his facade. Now take his voice: it was definite, harsh, rugged. He moved firmly, solidly, dressed quietly. 'You should appraise yourself', he went on. 'Your sleeves are too tight, your voice is too high and too

11

precise. You mustn't do it. It closes so many doors. It limits you unnecessarily ... I take ruthless stock of myself in the mirror before going out, for even a polo jumper or an unfortunate tie exposes one to danger ...'[9]

Danger seems a strange word for the most famous young man of his generation to apply to the public. But there were so many things about Coward that the English might misconstrue as bad show. He was brash and driven. He was hard working and infuriatingly precocious. He was homosexual. He was also largely self-educated and raised, as he wrote, in circumstances which were 'liable to degenerate into refined gentility unless carefully watched.'[10]

Coward watched himself like a hawk. As he allows Garry Essendine to admit in *Present Laughter*, Coward was always calibrating his effect, 'watching himself go by.'

In public, Coward's charm worked a treat. Coward himself liked to joke about the fine face he put on his celebrity. 'I was incredibly unspoilt by my success', he wrote in the first volumes of his autobiography *Present Indicative*. But in private, his panic sometimes showed through. Dame Sybil Thorndike remembered that Coward 'could play these nervous strange people, hysterical people, which is very rare ... He was absolutely wonderful. It's only people who are hysterical who can play hysterical parts. You see, he could *scream*!'[11] Coward was an upstart. To Edith Sitwell, whom he lampooned unmercifully in *London Calling!*, he was 'little Coward'[12] and even to the architectural historian James Lees-Milne, he was 'red in face, assertive, middle-aged and middle-class'.[13] Coward had to work hard at masking his ambitious self-involvement. His legendary charm couldn't hide it from everyone. Chips Channon recounts having tea with Coward in 1945: 'He was flattering (he is an arch-flatterer), insinuating, pathetic, and nice. I have never liked him so much, though he talked mostly about himself. At length, after many compliments and vows of eternal friendship, he left ...'[14]

Coward recognized his craving for acceptance as his greatest fault. In *Easy Virtue*, Larita Whittaker, like him a stylish outsider with a secret, admits: 'I've got an unworthy passion for popularity'. And Coward's self-avowed alter-ego, the romantic comedian Garry Essendine says, 'My worst defect is that I worry too much about what people think of me'. The craving for acceptance and its corollary, the hunger for fame, are, like any aspect of greed, irrational drives which can never be satisfied. Long before he attained stardom, Coward was cultivating the renowned, seeking admission into the aristocracy of success. In *Present Indicative*, Coward lists 36 famous people between 1917 and 1919 (among them Ivor Novello, Hugh Walpole, H. G. Wells, W. Somerset Maugham, Rebecca West) with whom he had either a personal or a nodding acquaintance. 'The list,' he writes, 'must make it obvious to the meanest intelligence that I was progressing like wildfire'.[15]

Always one step ahead of his generation, Coward was born on December 16, 1899. By the time he was twenty, he'd been on the stage for a decade. 'I was not in the least scarred by the war,' he wrote, having spent nine months in the Army, much of which was in sick bay. 'The reasons for my warped disenchantment with life must be sought elsewhere.'[16] His coming of age coincided with the emergence of Youth as a new, demanding force in English society. Newspapers continually mulled over 'the question of Youth'. Said one *Evening Standard* editorial (1924): 'Post War Youth won the war ... Youth ought to make the peace ... but mere noise, high-spirited defiance is no substitute for service'. Coward combined a Victorian work ethic with the hijinx of the young. He was industry in cap and bells. He layed siege to the public as songwriter, actor and playwright. He wanted to be everywhere. And because of his talent and the changing times, he largely succeeded. He *was* the young idea of the twenties – 'gaiety, courage, pain concealed, amusing malice'.[17] In him, Youth found a symbol and a boulevard spokesman: someone equal to their elders in sophistication, yet who made their own impudent disenchantment a star turn. 'I was', Coward observed, 'The belle of the ball.'[18]

Theatre histories usually have Coward vaulting to fame with *The Vortex* (1924). But as early as 1923, at the opening of *The Young Idea*, Coward's charm was infantilising an audience and inspiring something like a riot in a West End theatre. 'There were others', wrote the bug-eyed *Evening Standard* critic in a review headlined 'FIRST NIGHT LIKE A PARTY', 'who shouted "Noël! Noël! Noël!" in the manner of the pre-Trotsky Russian army celebrating Christmas old style. When some bright remark in the classic way of English comedy was made, somebody behind me said ecstatically "Another Noëlism". After somebody else on stage had worn a jazz kind of scarf, a party of people in a box whose horn spectacles set off their youth, hung quantities of scarves of the same material over the ledge.'[19] According to St. John Ervine, as Coward came out to make his curtain speech, a girl cried, 'It's a wonderful show!'[20] As Coward recalled that moment, he was already in full command of his charm, 'I made my usual self-deprecatory speech with a modesty which was rapidly becoming metallic,' he wrote, 'but which had the desired effect of lashing the audience to further ecstasies ...'[21] To admit the artifice, he'd learned by the thirties, was a means of magnifying its effect.

'The great thing in this world is not to be obvious Nicky – over *anything*.' Between the leaden sincerity of *The Rat Trap* (1918) and that line in *The Vortex* (written in 1923), Coward became a playwright and professional charmer. Coward elevated politeness to a form of delight. 'An extra politeness', he noted, 'which is not entirely real.'[22] Manners, as he displayed them, meant a happy resolution of tension, the imposition of the same bright and artificial symmetry on life as on art. The persona was irresistible, tinged as it was with just the right sparkle of bitchiness and self-deprecating wit. He streamlined his performance as he did stage dialogue, preferring innuendo to overstatement.

14

'Taste', he observed, 'can be vulgar, but it must never be embarrassing.'[23] Charm became his passport to social as well as theatrical success. Charm's allure was that it tested the boundaries of manners without overstepping them.

Coward's obsession with charm not only dominated his life but his early plays in which he explored the range of its implications. His first produced play *I'll Leave It To You* (written 1919) dramatizes the power of a fiction to bring success. Uncle Daniel arrives from South America and promises to leave his fortune to whomever of the feckless Dermott family makes good. The lie gets the youngsters going, and they all become successful. When Uncle Daniel's fiction is revealed, he justifies the con (as all performers do) in the name of generosity: 'I determined to spur you on to do something.' The children are at first disenchanted, and Uncle Daniel leaves. They finally relent, and he's asked back into their home. The curtain falls with Coward making the charm of Uncle Daniel's dissimulation irresistible. A telegram arrives. He's found gold in one of his mines. 'I'm worth thousands, thousands', he exults. The family gathers around him. 'Uncle! Did you send that telegram to yourself?' says one disbeliever, Sylvia. 'Yes!!!' he says on the play's last beat.

The Young Idea (1922) takes the notion of charade still further. Subtitled 'a comedy of youth', the play is about youth testing charm, and the power of that charm to create harmony. Coward took the part of Sholto, a boy of 21 who was the same age as Coward himself when the play was written. Sholto and his sister Gerda return to their father's English country house with a 'little mission': to lure him back to his first wife, their mother. With Coward, charm is always telegraphed by chic, the outward and visible sign of a desire to captivate. At Sholto's and Gerda's entrance, the stage direction describes them as 'beautifully dressed'. Their distinctive look is in contrast to the stilted Victorian repartee they play out as they greet their father:

SHOLTO: ... You can never guess how we have longed for this moment. We've –

GERDA: Don't break down, big brother.

But the father, George Brent, twigs to their send-up:

GEORGE (*placing a hand on each of their heads*): Little girl – sonny – may I call you sonny?

GERDA (*ecstatically*): Sholto, he's *got* us! (*Laughing.*) I knew he would. You owe me twenty francs.

Charm, first and foremost, is a performance; and Sholto and Gerda are charm incarnate. Coward introduces them as 'actors'. From the outset, these sparky outsiders display carefully tuned antennae for their audience. They know what to show and how to show it. They know when they are succeeding and when they've been 'discovered'. As Coward dramatizes their dissimulation, it is a subtle manoeuvre to keep their real intentions hidden. Gerda and Sholto exhibit the same irrepressible traits as their author – brash, precocious, mercurial. 'Don't assert yourselves quite so much,' admonishes George Brent before they join his stodgy house party. 'Be more retiring ... All I ask is that you behave yourselves moderately well and try not to grate on everyone.' Coward sets up a contest to let youth's charm have a field day.

Before Gerda and Sholto enter, Coward has established a bitter, discordant, charmless world. The talk between lovers is of being 'blatant', of 'obviousness'; and between husband and wife of 'rudeness' and 'disillusion'. Gerda and Sholto have walked into a hunting household which is hardly a home. Cicely, their father's second wife, is having an affair with Roddy Masters with whom she rides to hounds. George treats the affaire with cynical forebearance:

CICELY: Are you trying to insult me? to drive me to my lover's arms?

GEORGE: I fail to see the point of my driving you, dear, when you trot there so nicely by yourself.

Gerda and Sholto remain unshaken by all these obstacles. Their bad manners are a put-on: a method of exposing the deadly attitudes of others without being claimed by them. When faced with Roddy Masters – whom they suspect is Cicely's lover and who's been called to Jamaica to take over his dead brother's estate – they dance around him with po-faced wit:

> SHOLTO (*sympathetically*): . . . Jolly rotten for you. You say he was your brother? (*Shakes his hand.*)
>
> GERDA (*shakes his hand*): You'll have to cheer up and try not to think about it.
>
> RODDY: It is such a beastly long journey.
>
> GERDA: I meant about him dying.
>
> SHOLTO: So did I.

They are ruthless in their social impersonations. They can play at being intimate to get information about Cicely's affaire ('We must get sympathy at all cost', Gerda says, inventing a tale about their mother being an alcoholic to disarm one of the dowdy guests and win her confidence). They can be tactless in order to send up the vacuity of the company. Says one lady: 'She has no go in her, that girl. She borrowed the top of my Thermos, and never returned it. Shallow, very shallow.' The kids are all go, whirlwinds of artifice. They manipulate even their own father, trying to stir up romantic feelings for their mother by tempting him with visions of a vacation to Italy where they now live. He cuts them short. He has no interest in their mother and is content with the life of a country gentleman. He can't divorce Cicely as long as she stays with him. He talks of 'playing the game' and 'sticking to the rules'. But the one rule of charm's dissimulation is conquest, so Gerda and Sholto try to engineer Cicely's elopement. Just as Roddy and Cicely are about to elope (a scene observed by the two pranksters from behind a curtain), George appears to try and reason with his wife. His argument is persuasive. 'You're going abroad to restricted Colonial society, with a man to whom you are not married. Can't you imagine what hell it will be? . . .' Cicely's determination is shaken. At this moment, seeing their plan about to collapse, Gerda and Sholto try one last tactic. They kill her with kindness, begging their stepmother to stay.

> GERDA: We want you with us – we're going to stay here always –

Played in the same high melodramatic style with which they first tried to fool their father, their vows of loyalty instantly drive Cicely into the arms of her lover. Charm has won the day, but not the war.

Act Three has the little enchanters back in Italy, paving the way for the return of their father into the family. Here again, the two kids are asked to meet an American whom their mother (not knowing of George's return) has agreed to marry. 'We'll be charm personified', they promise her. And they are. The American is a sincere, somewhat charmless man whom they regale with outlandish stories about their pasts in order to drive him away. Although he sees through their game and calls attention to its amorality, they succeed. Their charm is finally triumphant. Charm engineers harmony and banishes every obstacle which threatens their (family) identity. Mission accomplished, Sholto and Gerda disappear. The stage is left to George and his first wife, Jennifer. The mood changes from satire to sentiment, a fantasy world beyond charm where life can be celebrated instead of having to be defended against. 'The only thing in the world that matters is Youth', George says at the finale, endorsing the playfulness of his children. 'And I've got it back again. I'm 21, and I want to laugh and shout and tear the house down! . . .'

The Vortex did tear the house down. Although Kenneth Tynan complained that the play 'sounds today not so much stilted as high-heeled',[24] *The Vortex* was a terrific literary leap for Coward. With the play, Coward pushed the bounds of boulevard naturalism as far as they had yet gone. The shock it created was the shock of recognition. The high definition of characters, the new edge to his dialogue, the brazenness of his subject matter were handled with a conviction as formidable as his persona. His obsession was still with charm. But having explored the shallows of the idea, he waded into the deeper waters of its politics.

The Vortex is about gaining and maintaining charm. The poignance and satire Coward brought to the dilemmas of Nicky Lancaster and his mother, Florence, as well as their entire 'charmed circle' rocked the English public. 'Our parents forbade us to go', recalled one Coward fan in a TV documentary about his work. 'There on stage was a young man taking dope; his mother having an affaire with a young man ... I mean it was absolutely horrifying. But to us it was a revelation.'[25] It was also the sensation that catapulted Coward into the firmament of international stardom. Overnight, Coward went from 'Boy Playwright'[26] in the newspapers to 'Noël the Fortunate'.[27] And the longing for adoration and enchantment which was the subtext of *The Vortex* was finally and forever resolved in his life. Coward's art drew the world to him. He was charmed, a star of free enterprise for whom all experience was capital and all life a reward. As he wrote:

With this success came many pleasurable trappings. A car. New suits. Silk shirts. An extravagant amount of publicity. I was photographed, and interviewed and photographed again. In the street. In the park. In my dressing room. At the piano. With my dear old mother, without my dear old mother – and, on one occasion, sitting up in an over-elaborate bed looking like a heavily doped Chinese Illusionist. People glancing at it concluded at once that I was undoubtedly a weedy sensualist in the last stages of physical and moral degeneration ... This attitude, while temporarily good for business, became irritating after a time, and for many years I was seldom mentioned in the Press without the allusions to 'cocktails', 'post-war hysteria' and 'decadence' ...[28]

19

Coward could never quite understand the fuss. 'The main characters in *The Vortex* drink cocktails, employ superlatives and sometimes turn on the gramophone,' he wrote in answer to the critics. 'Apart from these mild amusements their degeneracy is not marked. Nicky and Florence are certainly frail for the purposes of the play, but not to any hair-raising extent. Florence takes lovers occasionally ... I consider neither of these vices any more unpleasant than murder or seduction, both of which have been standing tradition in the English theatre for many years.'[29] Outrage was the price *The Vortex* paid for making the public think.

The subject of *The Vortex* is enchantment: the yearning to cast a spell and be under one. Florence Lancaster strives to maintain the charm of her beauty and her youth. Her son Nicky, as the audience learns before he enters, also 'loves being attractive'; and 'will be perfectly happy as long as he goes on attracting people'. Young and handsome, Nicky is afflicted by insecurity and nervousness which are signals of an unappealing weakness in his character. To bolster his attractiveness he seeks the desperate remedy of drugs. Narcotics are not an incidental bit of sensationalism, but an emblem of the longing for enchantment, for magical solutions both mother and son seek.

Between their cigarettes and superlatives, Florence's bitchy friends set out the problems before Coward introduces Florence and Nicky into the dramatic equation. Florence is 'ageing', Nicky is 'weak.' Both are trying to hide from themselves. 'It's too late now for her to become beautifully old', says Helen, the voice of disenchantment. 'She'll have to be young indefinitely.' When Florence enters with her twenty-four-year-old lover in tow, the extreme stylishness of her clothes indicates her compulsion to charm. She is dressed, the stage directions read, emphasizing her anxiousness, 'brilliantly almost to the point of being "*outré*." Her face still retains the remnants of great beauty'. As soon as she enters, Florence is putting Tom, a Guards officer, through his paces:

the little commands and responses that show others (and herself) that she is adored:

FLORENCE: Tom, give me a cigarette.
PAWNIE: Here are some.
FLORENCE: No, Tom has a special rather hearty kind that I adore ... Thank you, angel.

Florence wants to feel that her waning beauty still has the power to enthrall. Coward reiterates the point as soon as Tom has left the room. Florence looks into a mirror. 'I look like Death', she says, adding after a pause. 'Isn't Tom a darling?' Her anxiety and its antidote are yoked together in a sentence. She wants to believe her charm is potent. When Helen suggests that it isn't, that she is more in love with Tom than he with her, she replies 'complacently': 'He adores me – worships me – he's never seen anyone like me before in his life. I'm something strange ... exotic ...' Later, as much to reassure herself as Helen, she repeats her claim. 'He adores me', she says. Her affaire is a symbol to her of youthfulness. 'I've kept young', she says.

When Nicky arrives from Paris where he has been studying the piano (Coward rarely passed up a chance to get himself to the keyboard), he cannot really draw her attention to him. She is spellbound by her own charm. She gushes over her newest photographs and Tom Veryan's dancing.

FLORENCE: Of course, he needs knowing.
NICKY: So do I.

But Florence doesn't hear him, just as she doesn't really see him. Even the news of Nicky's fiancée hardly fazes her.

FLORENCE (*with determination*): I shall be charming to her.

In contrast to Florence's stage-managed magnetism, Nicky seems unable to make himself alluring. His mother won't break her date with Tom to celebrate Nicky's homecoming after a year abroad. When his fiancée, Bunty Mainwaring, arrives to meet the family, Nicky is already hankering to be under a spell, to do 'something violently romantic'. He talks of the 'agony of romance', of love at first sight.

> BUNTY: Your playing helped a lot.
> NICKY: I meant it to.

But in his own home, away from the piano, there seems to be no enchantment about him, only nervousness. 'You've got too much hysteria', Bunty tells him. He feels vulnerable, 'frightened sometimes'. At the curtain, Nicky is pushed away even from Bunty, going off in jealous pique and leaving her to reminisce with her old acquaintance, Tom Veryan.

In Act Two, Coward shows the spell weakening. The 'hectic amusement' of the house party dancing indicates a certain unease. Nicky's charm evaporates almost immediately when his 'magic' is stolen by Helen Saville, who snatches his 'little box' from his coat pocket. Something is also missing between Florence and Tom, who talk as they dance:

> FLORENCE: What's the matter with you?
> TOM: I don't know, I suppose I'm tired.
> FLORENCE: You're not usually tired when you're dancing with me.

Is she losing her magnetism? Florence fears so, and her conversational gambits hint at her panic:

> FLORENCE: ... I get so tired of it all, so desperately tired. *She becomes a little pathetic.*
> TOM: Talk about being different, you're different too –

She begins testing her charm. She's unhappy, she's worried about people putting Tom against her. 'They better not try,' he says. Tom's bravado placates her.

> TOM: I'd – I'd be furious ... And I'd let them see it, too.
> FLORENCE (*holding out her hands*): Tom –

But later Tom sidesteps Florence's invitation to dinner. Explaining about having to see his mother, Tom hesitates just enough so that both the audience and Florence understand it is a social lie. Cowards shows Florence's charm beginning to wear thin. She can't hide her emotions or win automatic deference from others. She argues with Nicky about how Bunty contradicts her, a sign of bad breeding. 'Who cares nowadays?' snaps Nicky, sounding the brash note of an upstart age, 'We've all got a right to our opinions.' Florence struggles to turn every encounter, even this quarrel, into bulwark for her fantasy. 'She seems to forget,' Florence replies, grasping at flaws, 'that I'm much older than she is.'

The enchantment has gone from both their lives. Bunty breaks up with Nicky; and even as they end their engagement, Nicky is filled with nostalgia for the charm of his mother's looks. 'Everyone used to go mad over her and I used to get frightfully proud and excited . . .' But Bunty and Tom are no longer spellbound. 'One gets carried away by glamour, and personality, and magnetism', says Bunty, explaining the spell to Tom in their brief heart-to-heart. They kiss, and when Florence discovers them, she goes both literally and figuratively out of control. Bunty won't leave or give her an explanation. And Tom's kiss is more than perfidy, it's a humiliating signal of the impotence of Florence's appeal. 'You kissed her – you kissed her – I saw you! . . . In this house!' She orders Tom out of her sight. When he leaves, 'suddenly realizing he is gone', Florence runs upstairs after him: 'Tom – Tom – come back – come back – '

Throughout Florence's tantrum, Nicky has played discordant jazz. The music, which he associates with enchantment, fades away as dramatically as his mother's allure. When Florence makes her humiliating exit, Nicky's hands 'drop from the keys'. Charm has vanished.

Enchantment, a word whose root is based on the hypnotic suggestion of song, aspires to mesmerize. Act Three of *The Vortex* dramatizes the emergence of the spellbound from the spell. Nicky enters his mother's bedroom determined to disenchant her and make her see clearly both him and herself. He admits his vision has been blinkered: 'For years

23

... I've been bolstering up my illusions about you.' The emphasis of his talk is on sight.

NICKY: Look at me.
FLORENCE: Why – what do you mean?
NICKY: You've given me *nothing* all my life – nothing that counts.

Florence, of course, resists Nicky's insistence that she is labouring under a delusion. She admits that Tom is her lover. 'I'm still young inside – I'm still beautiful – why shouldn't I live my life as I choose.' But Nicky's disenchantment has brought clarity of vision. 'I'm seeing for the first time how old you are', he replies. 'It's horrible – your silly fair hair – and your face all plastered and painted ...' The visage with which Florence controlled her world is now 'face downwards on the bed'. Having disabused Florence of her magical solutions, Nicky tries to rid himself of his own. 'Look', he says, and holds out his little box, which Florence now sees for what it is: cocaine. They set about destroying each other's methods of enchantment. Florence heaves the box out of the window; Nicky goes to her dressing table and 'sweeps everything off to the floor with his arm'. The illusion of omnipotence is (temporarily at least) shattered. They must survive by cooperation, not captivation. 'You're not to have any more lovers', Nicky says. 'You're not going to be beautiful and successful ever again – you're going to be my mother for once – it's about time I had one to help me, before I go over the edge altogether ...' Florence vows to change. 'Promise me to be different', Nicky repeats. ' ... We'll both try.' The curtain falls with Florence stroking Nicky's hair, the first real gesture of contact between mother and son in the play.

Defending his play in the first flurry of its notoriety, Coward spoke of 'lifting the veil'[30] on a particular side of English life. Certainly upper-middle-class English elders and their offspring had never before been depicted in such a stark way on stage. 'Poor, soulless, rotten 1924', moaned the critic for *The Daily Graphic* after seeing the play. 'There's some consolation in having grown up before the war. Some critics have complained that Nicky and Bunty are not true to life. I seem to meet them everywhere.'[31]

The Vortex enlarged the limits of what was theatrically acceptable. But Coward was no reformer. 'Dear boy', he told an interviewer of the New York *Times* in 1970, 'I have had a few causes. In *The Vortex* I did. There was a great deal of morality in that drama. I disapproved of elderly ladies having young lovers ... Do I have to have social causes. I wanted to write good plays, to grip as well as amuse.'[32] In the end, as in the beginning, Coward wanted to be a spell-binder. Charm was not only the subtext of *The Vortex*, but the object of the exercise. The powerful but pat finale of *The Vortex* typified Coward's route to theatrical success, the life-long pursuit of the middle-way between truth and ap-plause. The comforting symmetry of his play defused its desperation. The sense of foreboding, the jangled momen-tum of the Jazz Age, the spiritual impoverishment of a stratum of society were contradicted by a structure whose balance and proportion implied a benign and well-made universe. And the insistence on gripping and exploiting feel-ings encouraged hypnotic suggestion rather than argument.

The Vortex, which dramatized the dangers of enchant-ment and success, set Coward firmly on a lifetime's pursuit of them. Remembering his first-night performance, he wrote, 'I was all over the place but gave, on the whole, one of those effective, nerve-strung, *tour-de-force* performances, technically unstable, but vital enough to sweep people into enthusiasm.'[33] He was still charming them at the curtain call:

> At the end of the play the applause was terrific. I happened to cut a vein in my wrist when, towards the end of the last act, I had to sweep all the cosmetics and bottles off the dressing table. I bound it up with my handkerchief during the curtain calls, but it bled effectively through my author's speech ...[34]

In *The Vortex*, Coward had examined charm as something dangerous to pursue. In *Hay Fever* (1925), he tackled the idea from the opposite angle and dramatized the vanity in charm's dissimulation. The play's central character, Judith Bliss, is a well-known actress and the joke revolves around the spellbinder's awareness of her artificiality. She's invited a young man down for the weekend. 'He's a perfect darling, and madly in love with me – at least, it isn't me really, it's my Celebrated Actress glamour, but it gives me a divinely cosy feeling.' Almost as soon as the curtain goes up, Coward focuses on the politics of charm with Simon Bliss calling attention to his mother's role-playing:

SIMON: You were being beautiful and sad.

JUDITH: But I am beautiful and sad.

SIMON: You're not particularly beautiful, darling, and you never were.

JUDITH: Never mind; I made thousands think I was.

In *Easy Virtue* (1925), Coward tried yet another approach to his obsession with charm. In Larita Whittaker's losing battle with the rigidity of upper-middle-class English life, Coward tried to show charm as an act of moral courage. Larita, like Coward, is an outsider with an unconventional sexual past. Also like his Garry Essendine fourteen years later, she admits to the habit of 'watching ourselves go by' and the need to be popular: '. . . it hurts my vanity not to be an unqualified success'. The characters comment on her qualities. 'I haven't got Lari's beauty or charm or intelligence', says one character, about the divorcee who has met and married young John Whittaker in France. Larita is a model of style and taste. Her entrance at the end of Act One is in showy contrast to the stodgy and 'repressed' Whittaker women. As Coward describes her:

She is tall, exquisitely made-up and very beautiful – above everything, she is perfectly calm. Her clothes, because of their simplicity, are obviously violently expensive: she wears a perfect rope of pearls and a small close travelling-hat.

Larita is yet another study of flawless charm; and her first polite words to her frosty mother-in-law admit an understanding about disguising feeling. 'How-do-you-do seems so hopelessly inadequate, doesn't it, at a moment like this?' Larita says, taking both Mrs. Whittaker's hands. 'But perhaps it's good to use it as a refuge from our real feelings.'

Mrs. Whittaker represents the old guard; and Larita the new. Mrs. Whittaker is judgmental, self-righteous, and stiff. 'The stern repression of any sex emotions all her life', writes Coward in his trendy opening stage direction, 'has brought her to middle-age with a faulty digestion which doesn't so much sour her temper as spread it.' Larita, a divorcee with scandal in her past, is easy with men and money. She has a restless intelligence, and the charm of her flippancy allows her to say hard things bravely. Coward is at pains to show off Larita's charm at the end of Act One. His spare dialogue allows a mood, a glance, the handling of an object to convey Larita's confident sophistication. Charles Burleigh, a guest in the Whittaker house, offers her a cigarette. She refuses and takes her own.

She takes a cigarette out of her case.

CHARLES (*lighting hers and his own*): That's an enchanting case.

LARITA: It *is* a darling.

CHARLES: Cartier?

LARITA: No; Lacloche. I've had it for years.

CHARLES: Were you in Paris long?

LARITA: Only a week. I had to get some new clothes and fortify myself.

CHARLES: Naturally.

LARITA: Where is everybody?

CHARLES: I don't know.

LARITA: They're discussing their first impression of me, I expect. It must be horrid for them.

CHARLES: I don't see why.

LARITA (*smiling*): You do – perfectly well.

The exchange dramatizes not only Larita's appeal; but her ability to gauge the reaction of others to her. Her charm is a knowing sensitivity to the people around her. By the end of the scene, she and Charles 'both laugh a good deal'. Through charm, she promotes intimacy.

In retrospect, Coward maintained that 'Women with pasts today receive far more enthusiastic social recognition than women without pasts. The narrow-mindedness, the moral righteousness, and the over-rigid social codes have disappeared, but with them has gone much that was graceful, well-behaved and endearing. It was in a mood of nostalgic regret at the decline of such conventions that I wrote *Easy Virtue*.'[35] There is no regret in the play; and the only nostalgia seems to be for living high off the hog.

Writing as both a young Turk and a new man-about-town, Coward wanted entrée into the upper-middle-class milieu he set out to criticize. He doesn't so much bite as gum the hand that fed him. The result makes the play's debate theatrical but unconvincing. In Act Two, Larita's marriage is floundering after three months. She is bored; John is indifferent. Coward shows her indoors, swathed in a fur coat on a fine summer day, reading Proust's *Sodom and Gomorrah*. (This isn't so much a sign of her 'liberal-mindedness', 'decadence' or 'intelligence' as a veiled indication of the real sexual issue Coward tries vainly to raise in the ensuing debate about decency.) 'There are so many varying opinions as to what is straight and decent', Larita says to Marion Whittaker, a chip off the old block of ice who snubs her Proust reading, saying 'Pity he chooses such piffling subjects'. Sex is the issue of the play which neither Coward's nor Larita's charm will allow them to face directly. When Larita does try and tell her husband a heavy truth, she does it with stylish lightness.

JOHN: You're not happy here at all ... Why?
LARITA: Because you've stopped loving me.
JOHN (*startled*): Lari!

LARITA: It's true.
JOHN: But you're wrong – I haven't stopped loving you.
LARITA (*lightly*): Liar!

To make charm look like courage Coward allows Larita to be provoked beyond endurance. When she finally admits to anger, she says – in Coward's new fangled Freudian jargon – 'I've repressed it for so long, and repression's bad. Look at Marion.' Larita is forced to abandon charm, first in a fight with her husband to make him understand, then in a quarrel with Mrs. Whittaker to make her shut up. To John, she is appalled at her bad manners: 'I've shown myself to you as quarrelsome and cheap and ugly for the first time – and it hasn't hurt you; it's only irritated you. You're miles away from me already.' The combination of self-awareness and sincerity only combine to make her more charming. In the same way, when she argues with Mrs. Whittaker and loses control of herself, the moment only magnifies Larita's magnanimity. Mrs. Whittaker dredges up an old scandal to hound her with: a man had committed suicide and she had been held responsible for the tragedy. Larita makes a quick, definitive reply:

MRS. WHITTAKER: And how have you lived since this – this – scandal?
LARITA: Extremely well.
MRS. WHITTAKER: Your flippancy is unpardonable.
LARITA: So is your question ...

Larita fends off vituperation with wit. Branded as a wicked woman, she retorts: 'I've never had an affair with a man I wasn't fond of. The only time I ever sold myself was in the eyes of God to my first husband – my mother arranged it ... You approve of that sort of bargaining, don't you? – it's within the law.' In Coward's effort to make Larita heroic, he turns her into a whirlwind of 'insights', fortifying her with psychoanalytic prattle he passes off as perceptiveness. When backed up against the wall, Larita displays a severe and realistic critical nature that charm hides. She reminds Marion that she knows her better than Marion knows herself. And then Larita launches into one of Coward's now legendary finger-wags: '... All your life you've ground down perfectly natural sex impulses, until your mind has become a morass of inhibitions – your repression has run into the usual channel of religious hysteria.' In this fairy tale of charm denied, Larita is sent to her room and banned by Mrs. Whittaker from the big dance that night. The stage is set for the spectacle of Larita's vindictive triumph in Act Three.

Larita's entrance mid-way through the dance is sensational and meant to mesmerize. Her presence is brilliant.

> At this moment LARITA appears at the top of the stairs. Her dress is dead-white and cut extremely low; she is wearing three ropes of pearls and another long string twined round her right wrist. Her face is as white as her dress and her lips vivid scarlet. Her left arm positively glitters with diamond, ruby and emerald bracelets; her small tiara of rubies and diamonds matches her enormous ear-rings; she also displays a diamond anklet over her cobweb fine flesh-coloured stocking. She is carrying a tremendous scarlet ostrich-feather fan. There is a distinct gasp from everybody ...

Charm personified, Larita's appeal is also lethal. Marion Whittaker drops her glass of claret-cup. Mrs Whittaker is dismissed with a one-liner: 'I don't live according to your social system', Larita says. Every head turns. Every man registers the gravitational pull of her magnetism. Larita is at once sensational and knowing. She even tells one chinless wonder who asks for a dance, 'How much would you have won from your little friend if I had agreed to dance with you?' The point of charm is to protect oneself (and others) from hurt; and Larita negotiates a decent exit for herself. She encourages her husband's old girl friend, Sarah, 'to look after John for me', and promises a quick, quiet divorce. Charm helps her survive her solitude. She re-establishes the old enchantment as she's about to set out again alone. Her husband asks her why she's dressed like a Christmas tree:

LARITA: It was done with a purpose.
JOHN: What purpose?
LARITA: It was a sort of effort to re-establish myself – rather a gay gesture – almost a joke!

Decked out in her glamorous clothes, bags packed for The Ritz in Paris where she 'always' stays, Larita keeps firm hold of her charm when she encounters John just as she's about to leave him without saying goodbye.

JOHN: What's the matter, Lari? Why are you looking like that?
LARITA: I think I'm going to sneeze.

Larita leaves with no fuss and no explanations. Her defeat is intended to be made glorious by the charm of her good manners in the face of intolerable circumstances.

Coward, like Larita, loved being sensational and had learned how to hard-shoulder catcalls of depravity and decadence. Coward wrapped himself in his success. Having practised getting sympathy for his characters, he knew how to get it for himself. 'Please don't be in the least annoyed by Hannen Swaffer's remarks', Coward wrote to his mother in 1926. 'He doesn't worry me at all. The more frightful things he says the more sympathy *I* get and it doesn't matter what the papers say anyhow good or bad.'[36] When Coward's *Fallen Angels* (1925) – a very light comedy about two married women faced with the imminent arrival of a lover they once shared – was barracked in the press as 'Those Soused Sluts', Coward had just the right answer. 'The realization that I am hopelessly depraved, vicious, and decadent has for two days ruined my morning beaker of opium,' he wrote. 'I find I no longer enjoy my four o'clock cocaine tablets, and I have flung my hypodermic needle into the Thames with the firm resolution of turning over a new leaf and for the future I intend to write only the healthiest of healthy plays,

31

dealing exclusively with birth, marriage, and death in the open air.'[37]

Larita, and Julia Sterroll and Jane Banbury, the women in *Fallen Angels* who long for the enchantment of passion, are all the poor little rich girls whom Coward was also describing by then in song. In 1924–25, Coward had begun to sing about being spellbound. In the revue *On With the Dance*, he wrote:

> Poor Little Rich Girl
> You're a bewitched girl

True, 'rich' and 'bewitch' are as much code words to the boulevard as 'elf' and 'self' are to romanticism. But Coward had more to say:

> The role you are acting,
> The toll is exacting
> Soon you'll have to pay.

Having stormed the English public as actor, playwright, and songwriter, by 1925 Coward was selling it the sickness as well as the antidote. His charm became legendary. By the end of the thirties, charm was so ingrained a manoeuvre that it became a trap.

Present Laughter (written in 1939 but produced in 1942) is about the romantic comedian Garry Essendine and the politics of charm. In the play Coward admits the artificiality of his persona only to make its charm triumphant. Underneath *Present Laughter*'s high spirits is a dilemma: a man who dissimulates so eagerly that he has forgotten who he is. The issue is raised almost at once when Daphne, one of the spellbound who's wangled her way into Essendine's apartment for a one-night stand, is besotted by his charm. She talks to Essendine's secretary, who is disenchantment in a twin-set:

> DAPHINE: I think he's more charming off the stage than on, don't you?

MONICA (*with a slight smile*): I can never quite make up my mind.

When Essendine finally emerges from his room, bellowing like a baby being awakened, he launches into a romantic adieu for Daphne whose name he has long forgotten. He's a whirlwind of vanities, at once compelled to charm and exhausted by the power of his spell. 'Everyone worships me, it's nauseating', he says, slumped in a chair.

'Try not to be so charming', Essendine's secretary warns him. But he can't stop. His sense of ageing only heightens his compulsion to mesmerize. Almost as soon as Essendine is up, he's glancing in the mirror, assessing his waning allure.

GARRY (*taking a comb and going over to a looking-glass*): Good God, I look ninety-eight.

MONICA: Never mind.

GARRY: In two years from now I shall be as bald as a coot and then you'll be sorry.

MONICA: On the contrary I shall be delighted. There will be fewer eager, gently-bred débutantes ready to lose their latch-keys for you when you've got a toupée perched on top of your head, and life will be a great deal simpler.

GARRY (*thoughtfully*): I shall never wear a toupée, Monica, however bald I get. Perhaps on the stage I might have a little front piece, but in life, never. I intend to grow old with distinction.

Charm, originally a way of protecting personality, now substitutes for it. Essendine can't resist turning everything into drama ('This, to date, is the most irritating morning of my life', he says with typical self-dramatizing bravado.)[38] It's a good joke, and Coward uses laughter to show the audience the trick of his persona while enchanting them with it. When anybody corners Essendine with an uncomfortable insight about his personality (JOANNA: 'Why are you so afraid of being vulnerable? ... To be perpetually on guard must be terribly tiring'), Essendine artfully extricates himself

33

with a laugh-line or a set piece of hyperbole. Amusement becomes an anodyne.

Coward pits Essendine's charm against the adamant advances of two females and the arrogance of a would-be playwright. 'You were so busy being attractive and unspoiled by your success that you promised him an appointment', scolds the secretary, speaking of the imminent arrival of Roland Maule. Maule is flamboyantly charmless. His boorishness only magnifies and serves to vindicate Essendine's charm.

'I know you only play rather trashy stuff as a rule, and I thought you just might like to have a shot at something deeper' is Maule's opening gambit. He is hysterical, earnest, arrogant, gauche, and graceless. He has no idea of how to present himself, least of all to Essendine. 'All you do with your talent is to wear dressing-gowns and make witty remarks when you might be really helping people, making them think! Making them feel!'

Coward writes a 'charming' resolution to Maule's criticism which serves to reconfirm Essendine's boulevard self-confidence. Finally refusing to be polite, Essendine explodes and lays into Maule, only to find that Maule, too, has become spellbound. Maule, the stage direction reads, is 'hypnotized'. 'You're wonderful!' he says. Maule comes bounding back into the second act, determined to follow Essendine to the end of the earth and to ape his inimitable style. 'You see', Maule says, 'Every moment I'm near him I get smoother and smoother and smoother, my whole rhythm improves tremendously.'

Dissimulation, the subtext of the early plays, is the theme and central comic predicament of *Present Laughter*. The issue of enchantment has long ago been resolved, what remains for Coward is only the politics of manoeuvring his monolithic persona. 'Of course, Garry Essendine is me',[39] Coward told the BBC in 1972. Everybody tells Essendine he's acting. He's the first to admit it. 'I'm always acting', he confides to the eager Daphne, after she keeps interrupting a romantic set piece from Shelley. Then Joanna, the rapacious wife of his business partner who fancies the Great Man, tells him in Act Two: 'You are rather like a circus horse as a matter of fact! Prancing into the ring to be admired, jumping, with such assurance, through all the paper hoops.' Coward displays the power of Essendine's acting by fooling the audience, if not Joanna, by the force of his tirade against her.

GARRY: ... You want to know what I'm really like, do you, under all this glittering veneer? Well, this is it. This is what I'm really like – Fundamentally honest! When I'm driven into a corner I tell the truth, and the truth at the moment is that I know you, Joanna. I know what you're after. I can see through every trick. Go away from me! Leave me alone!

JOANNA (*laughing*): Curtain!

The chameleon will never reveal his true colours. Later, in the same superbly written scene, Essendine practises some of the romantic magic that has made him an star. Whether the emotions are real or false, Essendine brings a conviction to the moment that suspends all disbelief, even his own. Here, charm's game of hide-and-seek is irresistible.

GARRY (*prowling about*): How was the Toscanini concert?

JOANNA: Glorious. (*She sits down.*) He played the Eighth and the Seventh.

GARRY: Personally I prefer the Fifth.

JOANNA: I like the Ninth best of all.

GARRY (*casually sitting beside her on the sofa*): There's nothing like the dear old Ninth.

JOANNA: I love the Queen's Hall, don't you? It's so uncompromising.

GARRY (*taking her hand*): I love the Albert Hall much more.

JOANNA (*leaning against him*): I wonder why. I always find it depressing.

GARRY (*taking her in his arms*): Not when they do 'Hiawatha', surely?

JOANNA (*dreamily*): Even then.

GARRY (*his mouth on hers*): I won't hear a word against the
   Albert Hall.
   The lights fade and the Curtain falls.

Even Roland Maule embraces the notion of the performing self. He assumes Essendine is always acting, and so
nothing Essendine says is ever taken to be sincere. Essendine's real feelings are misconstrued as a charming put-on:
the persona is shown to be much more persuasive than the
real person.

ROLAND: ... After all there's no valid reason is there why I
shouldn't be acting being mad just as you're acting being sane.
GARRY: I am not acting.
ROLAND: You are always acting ... I am always acting too. I
have been acting mad with you because it amuses me to see you
put on a surprised face. I am absolutely devoted to your face in
every mood.
GARRY: I suppose you wouldn't like to act getting the hell out
of here, would you?
ROLAND (*laughing wildly*): That's wonderful!

'People', Coward noted in 1926, recuperating from a
nervous collapse, 'were the danger. People were greedy and
predatory, and if you gave them the chance they would steal
unscrupulously the heart and soul out of you without really
wanting to or even meaning to. From now on there was
going to be very little energy wasted and very little vitality
spilled unnecessarily.'[40] Charm was Coward's camouflage
that hardened into armour. Charm keeps the public engaged, and Essendine aloof. *Present Laughter* makes light of
this transformation.
   The play is Coward's justification of charm. It is one of
Coward's five enduring classics of light comedy because the
public, who pay to be enchanted, like to see charm triumphant. It confirms their sense of well-being and their faith in
manners. To elude his fans, Essendine tiptoes out of his
house, leaving them inside, polite to the end. The exit gets a

big laugh, and epitomizes the predicament of charm which lets people escape the responsibility of their actions. Coward allows Essendine to escape the enchanted, at least for the night. But Coward himself never did. The spellbinder is also trapped by the spell he casts.

2

Comedies of Bad Manners

'What is there to strive for
Love or keep alive for? . . .'
'Twentieth Century Blues' (1930)

'Ten years ago we were all looking for that "new world after the war",' wrote Ivor Brown of the twenties in the *Observer*. 'We had grand hopes of peace and plenty, of democracy fired by a common sympathy, of a new and kindly social order. People trumpeted the word "Reconstruction" as if it were magic. We had had our disillusions. Reconstruction withered where it grew . . . Bravery of thought was replaced by bitterness of mood. It was easy to doubt everything, hard to find acceptable faiths. The younger generation may have been dismayed; but at least it could dance. It turned its back on solemn creeds. It was light of toe, light of touch. Of that period and temper, Mr. Coward is the dramatist.'[1]

Long before Noël Coward put words and music to the twentieth century blues, he sensed the metaphysical exhaustion behind the twenties binge. 'Is this a game?' says one bewildered house guest in *Hay Fever* of the unrelenting role-playing that passes for purpose in the Bliss family. 'Yes', replies Judith Bliss with spirit. 'And a game that must be played to the end!'

Coward felt a loss of certainty and direction in English life. A society confused about its mission, the English sought refuge in fashionable distractions. In 1924, the night club was the newest symbol of the society's pursuit of pleasure; soon to be followed by the motor car[2] and the Charleston as totems of its fascination with distraction and speed. Short skirts and short hair signalled that women too wanted to be in motion. 'We're all so hectic and nervy', Nicky Lancaster said in *The Vortex*. There was a new momentum to English life; and the old social order as well as the strict codes of behaviour began to disintegrate with the acceleration. When Nicky Lancaster shut up his mother's twaddle about good breeding by saying, 'Who cares nowadays. We all have a right to our opinions', the battle lines between the old and the new worlds were drawn.

'For those who had grown up after 1918, the war was a memory, and soon hardly that,' writes A. J. P. Taylor in his *English History: 1914-1945*. 'In 1919 Rutherford foresaw the splitting of the atom, though he did not suppose that this could be turned to practical use. The theories of Einstein shattered the Newtonian principles which had given a rational frame to the universe. Freud shook, in a similar way, the rational frame of men's minds. The young began to steer without a chart. Even the praetorian guard of the established order turned traitor. Products of the public schools could no longer be relied on to remain conventional. The emancipation came first in private morals ...'[3] Coward's plays and revues were the stretch marks of this transformation.

In the introduction to his first volume of plays (1925), Coward mentions 'the present democratic destruction of all social barriers'.[4] Coward himself personified the myth. The son of a Teddington piano salesman found himself the rage of café society in London and New York, 'up to my arse in nobles'.[5] As Coward wrote, 'the imposing doors of the stately homes of England' were no longer 'austerely closed to the theatrical profession ... the cream of the aristocracy enthusiastically hobnobs with the clotted cream of the profession ...'[6] The equality of the theatre world was hardly an accurate barometer of English society, where one per cent of the population still owned two-thirds of the national wealth and three-fourths of the population owned less than a hundred pounds.[7] It was easier to democratize the stage world than the real one. And Coward did just that. His streamlined dialogue was a red flag to the John Bulls who thought his vernacular English subversive to their patrician world view. In the mischievous opinion of Somerset Maugham, Coward spearheaded the new naturalism that 'reproduced the average talk with its hesitations, mumbling and repetitions and broken sentences, of average people'.[8]

Although in later years Coward staunchly disavowed any reforming urge ('I rather cunningly kept it down'[9]), his earliest published pronouncement is full of renegade bravado about bringing the stage up to date with modern life. 'Is the theatre to be a medium of expression, setting forth various aspects of reality, or merely a place of relaxation where the weary business men and women can witness a pleasing spectacle bearing no relation whatsoever to the hard facts of existence and demanding no effort of concentration.'[10]

Coward saw himself as holding up a mirror to the manners of his age which was 'no more degenerate or decadent than any other civilized age, the only difference is that the usual conglomeration of human vices have come to the surface a little more lately, and there is mercifully a little less hypocrisy about'.[11] Sex was high on the list of subjects to be liberated from the prison of Victorian propriety, 'being the most important factor in human nature is naturally ... the fundamental root of good drama'.[12] Then, as now, sex was an issue that focused the disparity between the values of the young and the old, and for which Coward had been fiercely slated in the press as 'decadent' and 'depraved'. The subject brought out all Coward's strutting modernity: 'Rocks are infinitely more dangerous when they are submerged, and the sluggish waves of false sentiment and hypocrisy have been washing over reality far too long already in the art of this country.'[13]

But how to dramatize the change in the manners and the pace of English life? Coward's early plays suffer from a new sensibility mastering the old dramatic formulas. In 1921, after reading *The Young Idea* which has some similarity to his own *You Never Can Tell*, George Bernard Shaw warned

Coward not to see or read his plays: 'Unless you can get clean away from me you will begin as a back number and be hopelessly out of it when you are 40.'[14] It was good advice from a man whose theatrical life hadn't begun until he was well past 40. But Coward had to absorb his influences before he could discard them. Coward's gift was not for dialectic but for mimicry. He was still too young to put the new wine of his talent into new bottles. His early plays owed a great deal to Shaw, the well-made melodramas of Pinero and the epigrammatic clarity of Somerset Maugham. 'The *dernier cri* in the theatrical mode,'[15] wrote James Agate after the first night of *The Vortex*, seeing in the new voice a glance backwards at the old machinery of Pinero. *Easy Virtue* was also a homage to Pinero which Coward was the first to acknowledge: 'The form and tone and plot of a Pinero play was exactly what I had tried to achieve.'[16]

Coward came to see that the machinery and assumptions behind the traditional well-made play were inadequate for chronicling a society transformed by the World War.

From the 'Eighties' onwards until the outbreak of the 1914-18 War, the London theatre was enriched by a series of plays, notably by Somerset Maugham or Arthur Pinero, which were described as 'Drawing-room Dramas'. I suppose that the apotheosis of these was *The Second Mrs. Tanqueray*, but there were many others; *Mid-Channel*, *Lady Frederick*, *The Notorious Mrs Ebbsmith*, *His House in Order*, *Jack Straw*, *The Tenth Man*, etc, etc. There were also the more specialized Oscar Wilde comedy-dramas and the too infrequent, beautifully constructed plays of Hadden Chambers.

All of these 'Drawing-room Dramas' dealt with the psychological and social problems of the upper middle classes. The characters in them were, as a general rule, wealthy, well-bred, articulate and motivated by the exigencies of the world to which they belonged. This world was snobbish, conventional, polite and limited by its own codes and rules of behaviour, and it was the contravention of these codes and rules – to our eyes so foolish and old fashioned – that supplied the dramatic content of most of the plays I have mentioned. The heroine of *His House in Order* rebelled against the narrow pomposities of the family into which she had married. Lady Frederick, by gallantly and daringly exposing the secrets of her dressing table, deflected the attention of a young man who was infatuated by her into a more suitable alliance ... The unhappy Paula Tanqueray tried valiantly to live down her earlier moral turpitude, but ultimately gave up the struggle and perished off-stage in an aura of righteous atonement just before the final curtain. It is easy nowadays to laugh at these vanished moral attitudes, but they were poignant enough in their time because they were true. Those high-toned drawing room histrionics are over and done with ... The narrow-mindedness, the moral righteousness, and the over-rigid social codes have disappeared ...'[17]

Coward updated drawing-room drama by introducing both a new pace and new people. His characters are still rich. They are still an elite; but their status comes not only from birth but also from some exceptional quality of mind. A talentocracy mixes with the aristocracy. They use manners; but they are not bound by them. Instead of acting out the pre-war sense of continuity in English life, Coward's characters register the post-war isolation. They are, like the indulgent 'Children of the Ritz' in Coward's song (1932), 'only half aware/That all we've counted on is breaking into bits'. In the pre-war formula, the characters' sense of self is defined by society. But in Coward's best early comedies (*Hay Fever, Private Lives, Design for Living*), the 'exigencies of the world' no longer apply. The characters' worlds are defiantly private and self-obsessed. The pre-war drawing-room drama was built out of people acting against strict moral/social principles. In Coward's comedies, the drama is built around people testing principles. Unlike their plot-heavy antecedents, Coward's characters live comparatively plotless lives. Although Coward's comedies are well-made, the life they depict has lost its thru-line.

42

With *Hay Fever* (1925), Coward stumbled into a dramatic world uniquely his own. By traditional standards, the play was plotless: people arrive for a country weekend, they suffer through it and they leave. But within that simple framework, a new world and a new way of showing it was being discovered.

The Bliss family are ruled by no conventional codes of conduct. Stage language itself begins to stray from its conventional literary path and become what Maugham called, Coward's 'spoken hieroglyphs' where 'dialogue is eked out with shrugs, waves of the hand and grimaces'.[18] Maugham saw this as 'another nail in the coffin of prose drama',[19] limiting both the play of ideas and of wit. But for Coward this theatrical shorthand was to be a liberation: giving high definition to the surface of life on which he and his characters placed such great importance. Coward put on stage an actor's understanding of the theatricality of self-expression, how people communicate themselves in many ways besides words. Based on a weekend of word games and tantrums in the home of the American star Laurette Taylor[20], *Hay Fever* owes little to the influence of others, and everything to Coward's 'acute sense of the moment'.[21] But at first, the breakthrough seemed underwhelming.

> The idea came to me suddenly in the garden, and I finished it in about three days, a fact which later on, when I had become news value, seemed to excite gossip-writers inordinately, although why the public should care whether a play takes three days or three years to write I shall never understand. Perhaps they don't. However, when I had finished it and had it neatly typed and bound up, I read it through and was rather unimpressed with it. This was an odd sensation for me, as in those days I was almost always enchanted with everything I wrote. I knew certain scenes were good, especially the breakfast scene in the last act, and the dialogue between the giggling flapper and the diplomat in the first act, but apart from these it seemed to me a little tedious. I think that the reason for this was that I was passing through a

43

transition stage as a writer; my dialogue was becoming more natural and less elaborate, and I was beginning to concentrate more on the comedy values of the situation rather than the comedy values of actual lines. I expect that when I read through *Hay Fever* for the first time, I was subconsciously bemoaning its lack of snappy epigrams. At any rate, I thought well enough of it to consider it a good vehicle for Marie Tempest, and so I took it up to London to read it to her. Both she and Willie Graham-Browne were kind and courteous as usual, and listened with careful attention, but when I had finished they both agreed with me that it was too light and plotless and generally lacking in action, and so back I went to the country again and wrote *Easy Virtue* . . .'[22]

In Coward's other early plays, outsiders are always trying to infiltrate polite English society. Win or lose, the old guard remains intransigent and suffocating. The outsiders end up surviving anywhere but England: Larita Whittaker in Paris, Gerda and Sholto in Italy, Nicky Lancaster first in Paris and then tentatively in his mother's house.

In *Hay Fever*, the outsiders are at home in England. As with Coward, the Bliss family represent the new talentocracy of the twenties for whom the old hierarchy is no longer an issue. They are self-contained and self-satisfied. 'It's so silly of people to try and cultivate the artistic temperament,' says Simon Bliss raising the issue in the very first lines of the play, as he and his sister laugh at a friend's new book of poems. '*Au fond* she's just a normal, bouncing Englishwoman.'

In this new elite of talent, nothing could be more damning than to be normal. 'Abnormal, Simon – that's what we are. Abnormal.' Sorel is right about her family. Her mother, Judith, is a retired and much-loved actress; her father, David, is a novelist. Simon is an artist. They live by their own conspicuous 'slap-dash' code of behaviour. 'We see things differently', Simon says to Sorel, who would like to play by conventional rules. 'And if people don't like it they can lump it.' The Blisses imagine that they are free of the constraints of manners. But Coward shows that they have only substituted the rules of the bohemian world for those of the bourgeois world. To be interesting, to abhor dullness, to disdain normality, to indulge the self and its self-expression, to worship accomplishment are the rules which govern the Blisses' manners.

The eccentric and self-centred energies that in another era would have been thought 'off-side' and made the Blisses social pariahs now draw others to them. They attract a wide range of people. Sorel has a diplomat, Richard Greatham, coming to see her; Judith a fan, Sandy Tyrell, infatuated, as she says, by her 'Celebrated Actress Glamour'; and David has asked down a flapper, Jackie Coryton, to use for his novel, 'an abject fool but a useful type and I want to study her in domestic surroundings'. The Blisses make no bones about using people. They accept their egotism as part of their talent, and don't try to hide it. Thinking only of themselves, obsessed with catering to their individual vanities, the Bliss household rides rough-shod over everyone. When Sorel Bliss wishes out loud for some normal propriety, Simon reminds her of their heritage. Children of celebrities, they have been brought up to believe in the imperialism of the self.

SIMON: It's not our fault – it's the way we've been brought up.
SOREL: Well, if we're clever enough to realize that, we ought to be clever enough to change ourselves.
SIMON: I'm not sure that I want to.
SOREL: We're so awfully bad-mannered.
SIMON: Not to people we like.
SOREL: The people we like put up with it because they like *us*.
SIMON: What do you mean, exactly, by bad manners? Lack of social tricks and small-talk?
SOREL: We never attempt to look after people when they come here.
SIMON: Why should we? It's loathsome being looked after.

SOREL: Yes, but people like little attentions. We've never once asked anyone if they've slept well.

SIMON: I consider *that* an impertinence, anyhow.

SOREL: I'm going to try to improve.

SIMON: You're only going on like this because you've got a mania for a diplomatist. You'll soon return to normal.

Talent somehow mitigates the Bliss family's extraordinary behaviour. The Blisses may at times be vulgar and rude; but they are not stupid. They have some self-perception. Judith sees clearly that 'it's not really me' but her famous image that Sandy Tyrell is infatuated with. David Bliss tells Simon's guest, Myra Arundel, 'I write very bad novels'. What the Bliss family shares with Coward is a talent that isolates as much as it attracts.

'My sense of my own importance to the world is relatively small', Coward writes in *Present Indicative*. 'On the other hand, my sense of my own importance to myself is tremendous. I am all that I have, to work with, to play with, to suffer and to enjoy. It is not the eyes of others that I am wary of, but my own.'[23] As early as 1920, at his first press conference, Coward was announcing himself as his own solitary creation. 'I am related to no one except myself',[24] he said. The Bliss household exhibits precisely this isolating, asocial self-involvement. 'The Blisses' talent', the critic Ronald Bryden has observed, 'makes them impossible to live with, even for a weekend.'[25] Their private world must remain private because once their energies are artlessly unleashed in society the result is disruptive and destructive.

Manners are a kind of unspoken contract between the individual and the society which allows both to function efficiently. Harmony not honesty is required for society. Manners demand an individual put a rein on his more selfish impulses while imagining the feelings of others. The Blisses are constitutionally unable to do this. 'I'm devastating, entirely lacking in restraint. So's Simon', says Sorel who is trying to move in the worlds of the polite and the impolite.

'It's Father and Mother's fault, really; you see – they're so vague – they've spent their lives cultivating their Arts and not devoting any time to ordinary conventions and manners and things.'

When Judith Bliss makes her first entrance, Coward stresses her scatty vagueness, the first of her many hilarious self-centred idiosyncrasies.

SOREL: Clara says Amy's got a toothache.

JUDITH: Poor dear! There's some oil of cloves in my medicine cupboard. Who is Amy?

SOREL: The scullery-maid, I think.

JUDITH (*puts gloves on table and comes C*): How extraordinary! She doesn't look Amy a bit, does she? Much more Flossie. Give me a cigarette.

SIMON gives her a cigarette from box on piano.

Delphiniums are those stubby red flowers, aren't they?

SIMON (*lights cigarette for Judith*): No, darling; they're tall and blue.

JUDITH: Yes, of course. The red ones are somebody's name – Asters, that's it. I knew it was something opulent.

Judith's indifference to others extends to her own children.

JUDITH: It's too wonderful – when I think of you both in your perambulators . . . Oh dear, it makes me cry! (*She sniffs.*)

SOREL: I don't believe you ever saw us in our perambulators.

JUDITH: I don't believe I did.

Judith's observations, like everyone else's in the family, are self-centred. ('I should like someone to play something very beautiful to me on the piano', she says in the midst of the bickering.) Judith's proliferating imagination creates scenes in which she is the set piece. She is always watching herself. This self-referring afflicts each member of the family and results in the confusions of the house party. Is the Japanese room for Richard Greatham or Jackie Coryton? 'Oh no – it isn't,' Judith says, her scenario already in jeopardy. 'Sandy Tyrell is sleeping there.' And as for the punt on the river where Simon has visions of pitching woo to Myra Arundel, Judith declaims, 'I absolutely forbid it'. When the whole self-serving picture comes clear to Judith and she realizes that everyone in the family has invited a guest for the week-end without informing anyone, she immediately turns this act of separation into an image of community. She watches herself do the motherly thing, drawing her children around her in a stage picture which is a parody of good manners:

> SIMON (*comes over to his mother*): Mother, what *are* we to do?
> JUDITH (*pulls him down on his knees and places his head on her right shoulder. SOREL'S head on her left. Makes a charming little motherly picture*): We must be very, very kind to every-one!

Kindness in the Bliss family is out of the question. The Blisses make concessions to no one, not even each other. David wanders out of his study to announce, 'I don't want to be disturbed'. Simon admits to Myra, 'I love being diffi-cult'. And Sorel has already forewarned the well-known diplomat 'not to expect good manners'. They are by turns outrageous and apparently honest with each other. The vitality and humour in their personalities redeems them. Judith Bliss is the opposite side of the coin to Florence Lancaster in *The Vortex*. Judith's pursuit of young men is seen not as a tragedy but some kind of triumph. She is, at least, in touch with her emotions and herself. When Sorel scolds her for 'encouraging silly, callow young men', she replies: 'That may be true, but I shall allow nobody but myself to say it. I hoped you'd grow up a good *daughter* to me, not a critical aunt.' Judith is a mixture in equal parts of honesty and vanity. She can admit to her daughter that she envies her beauty, and then go off the rails fantasizing about her youthful image:

> JUDITH: Anyone would think I was eighty, the way you go on. It was a great mistake not sending you to boarding schools, and you coming back and me being your elder sister.

SIMON: It wouldn't have been any use, darling. Everyone knows we're your son and daughter.

JUDITH: Only because I was stupid enough to dandle you about in front of cameras when you were little. I knew I should regret it.

SIMON: I don't see any point in trying to be younger than you are.

JUDITH: At your age, dear, it would be indecent if you did.

Simon's last line to his mother echoes Nicky's in *The Vortex*, but with a difference. Nicky bolstered his 'illusions' about Florence; but Simon and Sorel are not enchanted by their mother's aura. They live in a world of art, and they understand about artifice. They tease their mother about her theatrics and love her preposterousness. She is an impossible and irresistible presence, emerging from every noisy family fracas 'buoyant, strong-voiced, restlessly and vulgarly alive'.[25a] Judith gives as good as she gets. About the imminent arrival of Myra Arundel, Judith tells Simon: 'She's far too old for you, and she goes about using Sex as a sort of shrimping-net.' And after Sorel cuts through one of Judith's melodramatic scenes calling her 'a lovely hypocrite', Judith takes a pause and says inconsequently, 'You're getting far too tall'. It's a daffy, dismissive *volte-face*. But Coward doesn't let Judith get away without criticism. What is fun for the family is hell for others. Judith likes to put a romantic cast on her selfishness; but the housekeeper allows the voice of normality to have its say. Judith orders beds to be made and meals to be cooked in her usual swanning, vague manner.

JUDITH: It can't be helped - nothing can be helped. It's Fate - everything that happens is Fate. That's always a great comfort to me.

CLARA: More like arrant selfishness!

JUDITH: You mustn't be pert, Clara.

CLARA: Pert I may be, but I 'ave got some thought for others. Eight for dinner - Amy going home early! It's nothing more nor less than an imposition!

49

On that note, with 'thought for others' still hanging in the air, the doorbell rings for the second time; and Clara goes to let in the first of the 'others'. By turns each of the guests arrives and is rudely treated by someone in the Bliss household. Sandy Tyrell is snubbed by Simon and Sorel, who refuse to shake his hand and exit abruptly. Myra Arundel, who has to open the front door by herself as well as lug her bags to the door, gets a cold shoulder from Judith. 'I've been mentally chilled to the marrow by Judith's attitude', she tells Simon who admits to feeling 'most colossally temperamental'. When Richard Greatham and Jackie Coryton arrive – 'those drearies' Simon calls them as he lets them in – they are left to languish alone in the living-room, after being 'rudely' scrutinized by Simon who takes Myra into the garden. The newcomers stand up out of politeness when Sandy and Judith come into the room, only to have them pass by without even an acknowledgement.

'I had been brought up by Mother in the tradition of good manners',[26] Coward said, and in *Hay Fever* he exploits his keen sense of social embarrassment. Good manners can't seem to negotiate a truce between the guests and the family. By yoking the flapper and the diplomat together, Coward is able in a few short strokes to convey two disparate attitudes of mind.

    JACKIE: Well!
    RICHARD: A strange young man!
    JACKIE: Very rude, *I* think.

When they go unacknowledged a second time by Judith, Jackie is close to tears, 'I wish I'd never come.' Always the diplomat, Richard tries to defuse the situation and replies, 'You mustn't worry. They're a very Bohemian family, I believe.' Richard's impeccable manners instinctively attempt to put Jackie at ease. He's prepared to do anything – even make a polite social lie – to give her some small sense of confidence. Coward shows this with masterly ease:

50

RICHARD: Have you ever been abroad at all?
JACKIE: Oh, yes: I went to Dieppe once – we had a house there
for the summer.
RICHARD (*kindly*): Dear little place, Dieppe.
JACKIE: Yes, it was lovely.

Manners are the guideposts of behaviour. And when manners are eliminated, human beings don't know where they are. Even Richard Greatham's confidence begins to crack.

RICHARD (*consolingly*): I expect tea will be here soon.
JACKIE: Do you think they *have* tea?
RICHARD (*alarmed*): Oh yes – they must.

When the tea finally arrives, it is, inevitably, a skimpy, self-service affair. The ritual coming-together turns into a tableau of isolation. The Blisses won't make polite conversation. They continue to be vague and uninterested in their guests. At sea in this inhospitable household, the guests cling to their manners like Ishmaels to their spars. There is an explosion of badinage between Richard and Myra who speak at once, only – as the stage direction reads – 'to both stop to let the other go on'. This politeness precipitates a silence, which in turn sets off another explosion of chat. The curtain to Act One falls on 'another dead silence'.

In Act Two Coward embroiders and inverts the game of manners. When the curtain comes up, the household is involved in an acting game called 'Adverbs', where each person is called upon to perform in the manner of the word. The game is about behaviour. In this brilliant scene, it becomes clear that the Blisses are expert at imitation, which sometimes tips over into parody. They appreciate every high-camp nuance. Judith takes a flower 'winsomely':

SIMON: Marvellous, Mother!
SOREL (*laughing*): Oh, lovely! (*Looking around the company.*)
Now, Myra, get up and say good-bye to everyone in the
manner of the word.

MYRA (*rises and starts with DAVID*): Good-bye. It really has
   been most delightful –
JUDITH: No, no, no!
MYRA: Why – what do you mean?
JUDITH: You haven't got the right intonation a bit.

Judith knows about intonation. The first time we hear of
her, she is studying the names of flowers, mastering the
vocabulary of the country house hostess. At the centre of
her talent, as Coward's, is a problem of language. 'The joke
of the play is the Blisses' misuse of a tongue alien to them',
Ronald Bryden observes, 'the clipped, stiff-lipped non-com-
munication of the English upper classes. They mock it, angle
and sharpen it, vitalize it with their own fantasy and intelligence: everything they say is invisibly in inverted commas.
They, and all Coward's comic characters, speak a language
of parody: they use the speech of the insiders like outsiders.
The brilliance of Coward's lines is their inability to take any
cliché for granted ... The humour depends on the tension of
imitation. The moment anyone *belongs* the language goes
flat.'[27] Parody is scepticism in cap and bells; and the Blisses
are sceptical about life. 'We none of us mean anything',
Sorel explains. And David puts the sense of absence this
way:

DAVID: ... I love to see things as they are first, and then pretend
   they're what they're not.
MYRA: Words. Masses and masses of words!
DAVID: They're great fun to play with.

But the guests don't understand any of the games the
Blisses are up to. They refuse to 'behave' like an adverb. No
amount of Judith's bullying will make them take part.
Finally, she falls back on the battle-cry of the well-bred to
'play up'. A family quarrel stops the game (SOREL: 'We're
a beastly family and I hate all of us'), after which the stage
is set for Judith to reverse her role and assume the mantle
of good breeding. She sets her hat at Richard Greatham.

'Will you teach me to be tactful?' she says. Within seconds, she is at the piano, playing a French song and being charming:

> JUDITH: Will you lean on the piano in an attentive attitude? It's such a help.
> RICHARD (*leaning on the piano*): You're an extraordinary person.
> JUDITH (*beginning to play*): In what way extraordinary?

Captivated, Greatham kisses her on the neck. And in a hilarious theatrical reversal, Judith becomes the histrionic model of conventional response:

> JUDITH (*dramatically*): What are we to do? What are we to do?
> RICHARD: I don't know.
> JUDITH: David must be told – everything!
> RICHARD (*alarmed*): Everything?
> JUDITH (*enjoying herself*): Yes, yes. There come moments in life when it is necessary to be honest – absolutely honest ...

Judith's mock decorum goes from strength to strength. She puts a well-mannered face on every tribulation she can manufacture. Having played the ingenue to Richard Greatham, she turns tragedian when she comes upon Sandy and Sorel kissing in the library.

> SOREL: Mother, be natural for a minute.
> JUDITH: I don't know what you mean, Sorel. I'm trying to realize a very bitter truth as calmly as I can.

Judith's performance is a way of passing time, of raising the amperage of life. If the company around her won't play, then she will. 'In the future,' she scolds Simon when the game collapses, 'we'd better confine our efforts to social conversation and not attempt anything in the least intelligent.' Role-playing races her imagination and allows Judith to live dangerously on her wits. The game takes control of her, and she can't stop. Rather than fight her mother, Sorel joins her:

53

SOREL (*suddenly*): Very well, then! I love Sandy, and he loves
  me!
JUDITH: That is the only possible excuse for your behaviour.
SOREL: Why shouldn't we love each other if we want to?
JUDITH: Sandy was in love with me this afternoon.
SOREL: Not real love – you know it wasn't.
JUDITH (*bitterly*): I know now.
SANDY: I say – look here – I'm most awfully sorry.

Judith ends up forgiving Sandy and offering him to Sorel
in marriage. Her histrionics reach their pinnacle when she
comes upon David and Myra embracing. Together they play
out an entire divorce scene with David promising to pay
Judith half his royalties and admitting 'You have behaved
magnificently'. Caught up in this bogus melodrama, Myra
tries to speak only to be hushed by David in the name of
good manners and social harmony. 'We owe it to Judith to
keep control of our emotions – a scene would be agonizing
for her now ...'

No intimacy, no emotion, no conversation, no vow has
meant anything. In the Bliss household, the world is merely
a laboratory for self-expression. They respect no conventional boundaries; they honour nothing but their imaginations. Nothing is significant to them except the Self un-
bound. The Bliss credo is 'I act, therefore I am.' For them,
reality is a vacuum which they fill up with their imaginings.
Their life is in play, not in the world. Coward artfully
manoeuvres his game to let the voice of normality be heard.
'This house is a complete feather-bed of false emotions –
you're posing self-centred egotists', Myra explodes. 'Every
time I opened my mouth I've been mowed down by
theatrical effects. You haven't got one sincere or genuine
feeling among the lot of you – you're artificial to the point
of lunacy ...'

Myra's salvo rallies the family. The moment is a brilliant,
hilarious bit of innovative stagecraft. Divided in play at the
beginning of Act Two, the Blisses are united in play at the

end of the act. They launch into a scene from Judith's old success *Love's Whirlwind*, recapitulating lines spoken in jest in Act One. Shouting, shrieking, they whip themselves up into a high-camp frenzy over the old Victorian melodramatic stage formula and its notion of respectability. 'She'll cry more, poor mite, when she realizes her mother is a – a – '. The moment never loses its light touch. It echoes the serious issues of parody, talent, manners, artifice and the shift in the English order of things that *Hay Fever* superbly raises. 'Answer me – is this true?' Sorel exclaims in character, but speaking the audience's question as well as the guests. 'Yes, yes!' Judith totters and falls in a dead faint. In a prophetic stage picture, the guests, like so much of the public in the twenties, look on 'dazed and aghast' at the hijinx of the new talentocracy.

In Act Three, Coward again pits convention against talent, as first the guests and then the Blisses come down for Sunday breakfast. In their exchanges, the guests tote up the list of social outrages. Sandy has been briefly engaged to Sorel, Jackie to Simon ('Judith gave us to one another before we knew where we were'). On top of that, Jackie reports that David Bliss didn't even remember her. 'I went into his study soon after I arrived yesterday and he said, "Who the hell are you?"' To this list of misdemeanours, Richard and Myra add other deprivations: bad food, bad accommodation, and apparently not even sugar for coffee. Manners are based on reciprocity, and that reciprocity between the Blisses and their guests never existed. Abandoning all sense of propriety, the guests decide to escape.

SANDY: Let's all go away – quietly!
RICHARD: Won't it seem a little rude if we *all* go?
MYRA: Yes, it will. You and Miss Coryton must stay.
JACKIE: I don't see why.
SANDY: I don't think they'd mind *very* much.
MYRA: Yes, they would. You must let Mr. Greatham and me get away first, anyhow . . .

In the next lot of negotiations, the guests take refuge in the manners that didn't work with the Blisses.

MYRA: Oh, you have got a car, haven't you ... Will it hold all of us?

JACKIE: You said it would be rude for us all to go. Hadn't you and Mr. Greatham better wait for a train?

MYRA: Certainly not.

RICHARD (*to* SANDY): If there is room, we should be very, very grateful.

No sooner have the guests gone up to pack, than the Blisses are coming down for breakfast. As usual, they are caught up in their own worlds. Simon arrives with his latest drawing. Judith is absorbed in reading tidbits about herself in the papers. Sorel is daydreaming about a South Sea idyll, and David announces he's finished his novel. He begins to read it and immediately the family is immersed in the geography of Paris and whether David's novel has got it wrong. Egos bristle and tempers are soon out of control.

DAVID (*loudly – banging the table with his fist*): I have *not* got it all muddled ...

JUDITH: It's so silly to get cross at criticism – it indicates a small mind.

DAVID: Small mind my foot!

JUDITH: That was very rude. I shall go to my room in a minute.

DAVID: I wish you would.

JUDITH (*outraged*): David!

There are 'tears of rage'; pages of the manuscript are thrown to the ground; fists pound the table; the children loudly take sides. Amidst this din, the guests creep down the stairway unnoticed. They reach the front door just as Judith reaches the top of her tearful aria. Sorel has told her to be quiet and sit down. Judith is 'wailing':

JUDITH: Oh, oh! To think that my daughter should turn against me!

DAVID: Don't be theatrical.
JUDITH: I'm not theatrical – I'm wounded to the heart.

The pandemonium ('They all shout at each other as loud as possible') reaches a crescendo as the guests slam the door behind them. The stage direction reads: 'There is dead silence for a moment, then the noise of a car is heard.' The sound helps Coward emphasize the Blisses' isolation. They are (and must remain) alone with their talent. One by one they sit back around the breakfast table.

JUDITH: How very rude!
DAVID: People really do behave in the most extraordinary manner these days –

In the next breath, the guests are forgotten. They return to their artistic pursuits. The curtain falls on David Bliss beginning again to read his novel.

Coward's joke at the finale is terrific. The final image brings the play full circle. The Blisses expect conventional courtesy while staunchly refusing to honour conventional behaviour. Coward ridicules this folly, but not without affection for the Blisses' eccentric energy. Manners allow individuals to face situations and provide a framework in which to act. But the game must be reciprocal. Otherwise, as *Hay Fever* so superbly illustrates, the result is chaos. A member in high standing with the talentocracy, Coward believed in the reciprocity the Blisses do not. 'The public are very fond of me. I've done well by them, given them a lot', he said. 'I'm proud that I'm popular and I've tried my best not to spoil it.'[28] In his laughter and his life, Coward mediated between talent and temperament, outrageousness and discretion.

But in *Hay Fever*, the first and the finest of his major plays, he gives malice and bad manners an outing. In so doing, the play not only chronicles a new caste in English life but a shift in behaviour. In the years to come, the Blisses' manners would prevail. 'Let [Coward] spare us more of these silly children',[29] pleaded the *Sunday Times*. But these silly children were the next generation of the well-to-do – a generation for whom Coward was both a spokesman and a myth. 'There is no one now writing who has more obviously a gift for the theatre than Mr. Noël Coward, nor more influence with young writers,' wrote Somerset Maugham in 1929, in an American volume of Coward's plays that included *Hay Fever*. 'It is probably his inclination and practice that will be responsible for the manner in which plays will be written during the next thirty years.'[30]

'In the twenties and thirties whenever I was about to do a new production in England I always used to go to New York for a fortnight and go to every single play because the tempo and the wonderful speed and vitality of the theatre was far superior to the English then,'[31] Coward told the BBC. Tempo itself was a metaphor of the changing, bad-mannered times. New rhythms brought new expectations and a more frantic sense of life. Coward was not above exploiting the old elegance as well as the new stridency. He puts the old and new tempos at loggerheads in *Bitter-Sweet* (1929) when old world comments on new, operetta on jazz. At a London society dance in 1929, where 'a swift jazz tune' plays and young couples 'jig about', Lady Shane puts a stop to the new sound and the new dances. She stamps her foot.

> LADY SHAYNE: Stop – stop – it's hideous – you none of you know anything or want anything beyond noise and speed – your dreams of romance are nightmares. Your conception of life grotesque. Come with me a little – I'll show you – listen – listen . . .

Lady Shane transports the youngsters (and the audience) back to the 19th-century world of romance, strict codes of honour, enduring loyalties, which contrast to the hasty allegiances of the girls and boys who sit listening to her. At the finale, when her story is finished, the youngsters 'all go jazzing out'. Lady Shane is left alone, laughing 'a strange, cracked, contemptuous laugh'. The laugh is meant to register loss and resignation. In her final reprise of 'I'll See You Again', the word 'goodbye' is a farewell not only to her memory of romance but to an age:

Though my world has gone awry
Though the end is drawing nigh
I shall love you till I die,
Good-bye!

The Depression put an end to the question of which set of values would prevail. *Private Lives* (1930), a triumph of personality and pace, caught the mood of dissolution. The bright, breezy veneer of its cross-talk hid disenchantment with a smile. The old narrative stage conventions had disappeared as well as anything remotely resembling the old values. Romance is a put-on, honour a masquerade, loyalty hardly an issue, communication a kind of truce between flying lamps. 'Within a few years', wrote one critic who had been vastly entertained by Coward and Gertrude Lawrence as Elyot Chase and Amanda Prynne, 'the student of drama will be sitting in complete bewilderment before the text of *Private Lives*, wondering what on earth these fellows in 1930 saw in so flimsy a trifle.'[32] Minimal as an art deco curve, *Private Lives*' form matched its content: a plotless play for purposeless people.

With its expensive moonlight and svelte quarrelling couples, *Private Lives* best embodies the Coward myth of chic dressing-gowns and bitchy dressing downs. He wrote it as a vehicle for himself and Gertrude Lawrence.[33] 'In 1923 the play would have been written and typed within a few days of my thinking of it,' he wrote. 'But in 1929 I had learned the wisdom of not welcoming a new idea too ardently, so I forced it into the back of my mind.'[34] He thought about it a long time and finally knocked it out in four days while recovering from flu in Shanghai. 'I thought it was a shrewd and witty comedy, well-constructed on the whole, but psychologically unstable; however, its entertainment value seemed obvious enough, and its acting opportunities for Gertie and me admirable ...'[35] Always the showman, Coward's instinct was for impact, not art. Later, Coward came to see that his enduring comedy was jerry-built.

> It is a reasonably well-constructed duologue for two experienced performers, with a couple of extra puppets thrown in to assist the plot and to provide contrast. As a complete play, it leaves a lot to be desired, principally owing to my dastardly and conscienceless behaviour towards Sybil and Victor, the secondary characters. These, poor things, are little better than ninepins, lightly wooden, and only there at all to be repeatedly knocked down and stood up again. Apart from this, *Private Lives*, from the playwright's point of view may or may not be considered interesting, but at any rate, from the point of view of technical acting, it is very interesting indeed.[36]

Private Lives allowed the Coward–Lawrence team to exploit their showy intimacy. 'She was so swift', Coward said of Gertrude Lawrence's comedy acting. 'And her eyes were so true.'[37] The dialogue called on their resources of quick wit and charm to create the illusion of spontaneity. 'I could not always tell', T. E. Lawrence wrote to Coward after seeing the play, 'when you were acting and when talking to one another.'[38] Coward's play gave his performing self more room to manoeuvre. Flippancy rules. 'As far as I know, this situation is entirely without precedent. We have no prescribed etiquette to fall back upon. I shall continue to be flippant.' Their swaggering selfishness isolates them:

> ELYOT: You have no faith, that's what's wrong with you.
> AMANDA: Absolutely none.
> ELYOT: Don't you believe in – ? (*He nods upwards*)
> AMANDA: No, do you?
> ELYOT (*shaking his head*): No. What about – ? (*Points downwards*)
> AMANDA: Oh dear no.
> ELYOT: Don't you believe in anything?

AMANDA: Oh yes, I believe in being kind to everybody, and giving money to old beggar-women, and being as gay as possible.

Once married and now divorced, Amanda and Elyot meet up again on their new honeymoons after five years. Each is hitched to a dullard. They decide to run away together to Paris. Not even stigma can stop them from indulging their passion.

AMANDA: ... we look like being in the hell of a mess socially.
ELYOT: Who cares?

As the title of the play insists, their world is private. Public concerns never intrude on them. They believe only in themselves; and their talk is unremittingly self-obsessed. And when they do register contact with the outside world, it is only dimly apprehended.

ELYOT: ... I went round the world you know after –
AMANDA (*hurriedly*): Yes, yes, I know. How was it?
ELYOT: The world?
AMANDA: Yes.
ELYOT: Oh, highly enjoyable.
AMANDA: China must be very interesting.
ELYOT: Very big, China.
AMANDA: And Japan –
ELYOT: Very small.

In the glib repartee of Elyot and Amanda can be heard the egotism of the talentocracy in *Hay Fever* which, over the intervening years, has seeped out into the world at large.[39] Elyot and Amanda have no apparent talent; but all the familiar inclinations of the new caste to indulge their individuality. Coward introduces these pretensions with bold, mathematical symmetry as first Elyot, then Amanda appear on adjacent Riviera patios with their new spouses. Both strain under the prospect of another conventional marriage. The scenes counterpoint each other, recapitulating the same newly-married badinage, the same jealousies, the same resignations, sometimes even the same words from both couples. A clear picture of Elyot's and Amanda's turbulent first marriage is evoked. What they both share, even before they encounter each other, is a secret longing for the Self to be extraordinary and omnipotent. Both vehemently argue that their divorce was the fault of the other. 'Are you going to understand me, and manage me', Elyot says to Sybil, already nostalgic for his freedom. 'Run me without my knowing it?'

Both Amanda and Elyot see their new marriages as dull, well-mannered routines. Amanda tells Victor, 'I've never felt less wild in my life. A little strained, I grant you, but that's the newly married atmosphere. Honeymooning is a very over-rated amusement.' And later she tells him: 'I love you much more calmly'. Elyot's love of Sybil is also different. He tries to convince himself that the detachment he feels is maturity. 'Love is no use unless it's wise, and kind, and undramatic. Something steady and sweet, to smooth out your nerves when you're tired. Something tremendously cosy; and unflurried by scenes and jealousies. That's what I want, what I've always wanted really, Oh my dear, I do hope it's not going to be dull for you ...' But Elyot and Amanda also see themselves as somehow out of the ordinary. Despite Amanda's promiscuity, Elyot has allowed himself to be divorced for cruelty and flagrant infidelity because 'it would not have been the action of a gentleman, whatever that may mean'. Amanda is more to the point about being extraordinary:

VICTOR: I'm glad I'm normal.
AMANDA: What an odd thing to be glad about. Why?
VICTOR: Well, aren't you?
AMANDA: I'm not sure I'm normal ... I'm so apt to see things the wrong way round.
VICTOR: What sort of things.
AMANDA: Morals. What one should do and what one shouldn't.

62

Elyot and Amanda soon fight with their new mates. In Coward's adroit traffic plan, the champagne cocktails, the evening dress, and the warring old lovers are quickly manoeuvred together on the patio. The scene is one of Coward's most memorable, setting down in its spare malicious banter the 'jagged sophistication' that became the vinegar in which the myth of the twenties is pickled.

AMANDA: Give me one for God's sake.

ELYOT (*hands her his case laconically*): Here.

AMANDA (*with a cigarette*): I'm in such a rage.

ELYOT (*lighting up*): So am I.

AMANDA: What are we to do?

ELYOT: I don't know.

AMANDA: Whose yacht is that?

ELYOT: The Duke of Westminster's I expect. It always is.

AMANDA: I wish I were on it.

ELYOT: I wish you were too.

Coward knew, as Elyot does at the baby grand in Act Two, how to manage the 'big romantic stuff'. He teased the moment, played coolly against it, built a sense of romance by delaying its fulfilment. His characters make their feelings clear while loudly denying their interest.

ELYOT: How old is dear Victor?

AMANDA: Thirty-four, or five; and Sibyl?

ELYOT: I blush to tell you, only twenty-three.

AMANDA: You've gone a mucker alright.

ELYOT: I shall reserve my opinion of your choice until I've met dear Victor.

AMANDA: I wish you wouldn't go on calling him 'Dear Victor'. It's extremely irritating.

ELYOT: That's how I see him. Dumpy, and fair, and very considerate, with glasses. Dear Victor.

Nowhere before this scene (and nowhere after it) is Coward's dialogue so oblique, so teasing, so bold in foreshadowing the new naturalism which the next generation of English playwrights would call 'the drama of the unspoken'. Coward brings to the moment both a professional and private understanding of innuedo. Coward the actor understands about subtext: the difference between what words say and the need they conceal. Here language is a decoy, what goes unsaid is as articulate and important as what is spoken. Coward the lover knows that too much talk about feeling kills romance:

> I am no good at love
> My heart should be wise and free
> I kill the unfortunate golden goose
> Whoever it may be
> With over-articulate tenderness
> And too much intensity ...[40]

In this scene both instincts combine to make Coward's sense of containment in life and language sensational. Maugham thought that such 'slangy, clipped and broken speech' made the playwright's task more difficult by 'narrowing the range of characters the dramatist can deal with' and 'restricting his themes'[41] since naturalistic dialogue could not deal with complexity of ideas. But Coward's gift was for dramatizing behaviour, not ideas. Far from 'killing comedy'[42] as Maugham prophesied, Coward's innovations in stage dialogue widened the nuance in staged behaviour and the stage's essential playfulness. Despite the patina of sophistication in Elyot's and Amanda's oblique repartee, what Coward creates in the scene is an elegant game of hide and seek.

These sleek figures (Elyot is 'slim and pleasant looking'; Amanda is 'quite exquisite with a gay face and a perfect figure') have the same carefully manufactured irresistibility as the dialogue. *Private Lives'* antics bear out Evelyn Waugh's dictum, 'Manners are especially the need of the plain. The pretty can get away with anything.' Even Elyot's and Amanda's monstrousness is charming. Coward presents the affectionate vindictiveness of their romance in such a

64

way that the audience expects them, wants them, to be extraordinary. And they are: extraordinarily silly, foolish, cruel and bad-mannered. Coward makes the point adroitly just as Amanda and Elyot are about to bolt from their honeymoons and disappear without explanation to Paris.

> AMANDA: Darling, I daren't, it's too wicked of us, I simply daren't.
> ELYOT (*seizing her in his arms and kissing her violently*): Now will you behave?

At a stroke, behaviour and the world of manners which govern it are turned upside down.

'There is no further plot and no further action after Act One, with the exception of the rough and tumble at the curtain of Act Two'[43] Coward wrote, describing the theatrical no-man's-land the actors who play Elyot and Amanda have to negotiate in the long expanse of conversation that fills the second act. Between Act Two's placid beginning and its brawling finale, Coward provides Elyot and Amanda with a little romantic flimflammery: a song at the piano, a foxtrot over the parquet floor. Act Two is about Elyot and Amanda trying to preserve good manners with each other. When old jealousies and recriminations bubble to the surface, they silence them with their code word 'Sollocks'; and harmony is momentarily restored. They gush charm, but they can't quite enchant each other with their perfect manners. Elyot tries to talk Amanda into bed, but she refuses because it's too soon after dinner:

> ELYOT (*jumping up rather angrily*): You really do say the most awful things.
> AMANDA (*tidying her hair*): I don't see anything particularly awful about that.
> ELYOT: No sense of glamour, no sense of glamour at all.

Amanda can't quite lose herself in love. 'Big romantic stuff', she quips after Elyot sings 'Some Day I'll Find You', his eyes riveted to hers. And later, when the squabbling starts to get the better of them, the dialogue comes back to the flagging spell:

> AMANDA *sits down on the sofa, and, taking a small mirror from her bag, gazes at her face critically, and then uses some lipstick and powder* ...
> ELYOT: Going out somewhere dear?
> AMANDA: No, just making myself fascinating for you.
> ELYOT: That reply has broken my heart.
> AMANDA: The woman's job is to allure the man. Watch me a minute will you?
> ELYOT: As a matter of fact that's perfectly true.
> AMANDA: Oh, no, it isn't.
> ELYOT: Yes it is ...
> AMANDA: It doesn't seem to have worked such wonders with you.

Inevitably Amanda and Elyot exhibit Coward's own characteristic self-consciousness in love:

> I am no good at love ...
> For I feel the misery of the end
> In the moment that it begins
> And the bitterness of the last good-bye
> Is the bitterness that wins.[44]

Amanda and Elyot talk a lot about passion and assume that their bickering proves it. But it also shows their separation from each other. They can't get outside themselves. They are too well-defended to share. The noisy torment they inflict on each other only serves to show the triumph of self-absorption over affection. What is going on underneath the surface of this Act is dialogue that has other implications. Elyot and Amanda's outrageousness is used to propound the aesthetics of high camp – an essentially homosexual comic vision of the world that justifies detachment. Everything that is 'bad' is 'good'. The play is serious about the frivolous, and frivolous about the serious. Says Elyot, 'seriously': 'You mustn't be serious my dear, it's just what they want'.

'Detachment', Susan Sontag writes in her 'Notes On Camp', 'is the prerogative of an elite'.[45] Elyot and Amanda are dandies of detachment. Elyot shows off his flippancy, Amanda her sexual nonchalance. Elyot, as he so often repeats, does not care about anything. Even he and Amanda are a cosmic giggle. 'We're figures of fun', he tells her. His flippancy ('Let's be superficial and pity the poor Philosophers . . .') is not an attitude of indifference but of philosophical detachment.

AMANDA: Darling. I believe you're talking nonsense.
ELYOT: So is everyone else in the long run . . .

In his early twenties lyrics, Coward sometimes expressed his sense of life as charade: 'Life is nothing but a game of make believe' ('When My Ship Comes Home'); 'I treat my whole existence as a game' ('Cosmopolitan Lady'). *Hay Fever* dramatized the notion of life as theatre, being-as-playing-a-role. *Private Lives* uses a heterosexual relationship to dramatize a camp sensibility. What in real life would be a tragedy becomes in *Private Lives* a comedy of emotional under-involvement. The point is made at the cosy beginning of Act Two:

AMANDA: It's nice, isn't it?
ELYOT: Strangely peaceful. It's an awfully bad reflection on our characters. We ought to be absolutely tortured with conscience.
AMANDA: We are, every now and then . . .
ELYOT: You're even more ruthless than I am.

Coward's frivolity is a serious strategy for avoiding the stalemate of conventional manners and meanings. To dethrone the serious, to neutralize moral indignation, to promote playfulness, to show irony in action is what Elyot and high camp want to accomplish. Wilde teased Edwardian society with 'bunburying' and homosexual code words of his own in *The Importance of Being Ernest*; and in 1930, Coward could go farther. But not too far. There is still no whiff of the real emotional issue under all the romantic bravado. Elyot and Amanda talk about transgressing the norms of society; but they act pretty much within them. They strain against convention but have no appetite for flying in its face:

> ELYOT: What shall we do if they suddenly walk in on us?
> AMANDA: Behave exquisitely.

Of course, when Sybil and Victor do walk in on the scene at the end of Act Two, Elyot and Amanda are rolling about on the floor in the last seconds of their ferocious free-for-all. The room is strewn with broken records, overturned tables and lamps. 'Beast', Amanda screams at Elyot before slamming off-stage, 'brute; swine; cad; beast; brute; devil – '. Coward's battle between the sexes is also a comic image of strangulation. In their 'paroxysm of rage', Amanda and Elyot don't notice the new arrivals. They bang off-stage into separate rooms: as isolated from each other in hatred as they were in happiness.

In *Private Lives*, Coward's device is to set up a series of expectations and then systematically reverse them. In Act One, the honeymooners end up running off together. In Act Two, the romantic idyll turns into a malicious brawl. In Act Three, Victor and Sybil's first horrified reaction to the scene becomes their fate.

> SYBIL: I'd no idea anyone ever behaved like that; it's so disgusting, so degrading. Elli of all people – oh dear. (*She almost breaks down, but controls herself.*)
> VICTOR: What an escape you've had.
> SYBIL: What an escape we've both had.

At the finale, of course, it is Elyot and Amanda who escape; and Victor and Sybil who claw away at each other. But when Amanda makes her first Act Three entrance just after this exchange between Victor and Sybil, she is fortified with good manners.

VICTOR: I must talk to you.
AMANDA: Well, all I can say is, it's very inconsiderate.

At her entrance Amanda is 'gracefully determined to rise above the situation', but her good manners soon harden from a protective mechanism into an offensive weapon. She makes inane small talk, staunchly refusing to discuss anything seriously while at the same time snubbing Elyot. Coward keeps up the discussion of the politics of manners by having Elyot sarcastically observe:

ELYOT: ... What manner. What poise. How I envy it. To be able to carry off the most embarrassing situation with such tact, and delicacy, and above all – such subtlety. Go on Amanda, you're making everything so much easier. We shall be playing Hunt the Slipper in a minute.

Elyot himself clings to his flippancy because he finds 'no form of etiquette to fall back on'. As he presents it, flippancy is a form of manners – a way of defusing a perplexing situation, a solvent for morality, 'no worse', as he says to Victor, 'than bluster and invective'. Flippancy 'hides a very real embarrassment', and therefore allows Elyot some room to manoeuvre without altogether abandoning his individuality. 'If you don't stop your damn flippancy', Victor says gravely, 'I'll knock your block off'. Victor tries to pick a fight with Elyot; but it's no use. Flippancy itself is an admission of exhaustion and disenchantment with any ideal, even the most traditional male role. 'All this belligerency is very right and proper and highly traditional', Elyot tells him. Victor is traditional. He wants reparation. He asks conventional questions and wants Elyot to adopt a conventional position. 'What do you intend to do? That's what I want to know', Victor says. 'What do you intend to do?' Elyot answers him with the 'sudden seriousness' that lies behind his flippancy. 'I don't know, I don't care.'

Coward neatly develops variations on this theme. Elyot's spat with Victor is followed by Amanda's with Sybil. Elyot ends up calling Victor a 'rampaging gas bag' and stalking off. Amanda loses her composure with Sybil. She sinks from the grandly dismissive ('I think you'd better go away somewhere') to the downright irritable ('Oh, go to hell'). Coward recapitulates the symmetry again in the ensuing discussions about divorce. First Victor and Amanda talk. After swallowing some humble pie (AMANDA: '... I'm a bad lot ... I'm thoroughly unprincipled; Sybil was right!'), Amanda and Victor agree to separate. She'll go her own way, and 'let the lawyers deal with the whole thing'. When Sybil enters after off-stage negotiations with Elyot, she announces that they are not going to divorce for a year. Having let out parallel story lines, Coward neatly reels them in with a joke.

AMANDA: It all seems very amicable.
SYBIL: It is, thank you.
AMANDA: I don't wish to depress you, but Victor isn't going to divorce me either.
ELYOT (*looking up sharply*): What!
AMANDA: I believe I asked you once before this morning, never to speak to me again.
ELYOT: I only said 'What'. It was a general exclamation denoting extreme satisfaction.

The temporary truce ('Sybil has behaved like an angel', Elyot says 'defiantly' to Amanda about Sybil) is signalled with breakfast where the warring Prynnes and Chases break bread together. But Coward uses the communal occasion for one last twist of the fun machine. Victor and Sybil start to quarrel. What starts the bickering is the very issue of flippancy which has separated Elyot and Amanda from their spouses. In the previous scene, Victor has tried to force Amanda, as he did Elyot, to be serious:

VICTOR: Why won't you be serious for just one moment?
AMANDA: I've told you, it's no use.

70

Flippancy draws Elyot and Amanda together at the finale, while dividing their partners against each other. Amanda ends a long polite soliloquy on the joys of travel saying '. . . then the most thrilling thing of all, arriving at strange places, and seeing strange people and eating strange foods – ' At which point Elyot chimes in: 'And making strange noises afterwards.' The line makes Amanda laugh, and she chokes on her food. The moment turns the emotional balance of the play. Elyot's and Amanda's bond is in the unprincipled, ruthless antic world of frivolity, a world delightful to inhabit on stage but dangerous in life. Victor immediately ticks off Elyot: 'You waste too much time trying to be funny.' Sybil replies that Victor has no sense of humour. 'I fail to see what humour there is in incessant trivial flippancy', Victor says. While Sybil defends him, Elyot winks at Amanda. (In *Design for Living*, Leo asks: 'Doesn't the eye of Heaven mean anything to you?' and Gilda replies: 'Only when it winks'.) Elyot's wink signals their bond in frivolity. Amanda smiles back at him. As Victor and Sybil's argument escalates into personal recrimination, Elyot grabs Amanda's wrist to stop her from interfering. She 'lets her hand rest in his'. The fight continues with Elyot blowing 'a lingering kiss' to Amanda amidst the brouhaha. As the war of words turns physical, Elyot and Amanda go hand in hand toward the door. They 'go smilingly out of the door' as Victor begins to throttle Sybil, and the curtain falls.

Coward ends *Private Lives* (as well as *Hay Fever*, *Present Laughter* and *Blithe Spirit*) with characters walking away from chaos. These stage pictures give form to the main mission of his laughter: frivolity aspires not so much to evade the issue as escape it. In *Design for Living* (1932), Coward raises the stakes of egotism and escape to their limit. The play enacts an attitude Coward put into song the same year in 'Let's Live Dangerously' from the revue *Words and Music*:

71

Let's live turbulently, turbulently, turbulently
Let's add something to the history of man,
Come what may
We'll be spectacular
And say 'Hey! Hey!'
In the vernacular ...
Let's live boisterously, boisterously, roisterously
Let's lead moralists the devil of a dance ...

The youthful, cruel high spirits of the song are at the centre of the hijinks in the ménage à trois of Gilda, Leo and Otto who torture each other with their comings and goings. In *Design for Living*, escape is both the issue and the limitation of the play. Commenting on Coward's attempt to mix serious statement and fooling, *The Times* observed: 'It is not a question only of mixing conventions: it is almost a question of running away'.[46] In its bid to be sensational, *Design for Living* is told in a style that isn't so much kiss and tell as admit and run.

As a star, Coward knew better than to let fame's greed show. 'If you're a star', he said, 'you should behave like one. I always have'.[47] In play, he could admit his selfishness; and it gives his youthful comedies their special heady amperage. Instead of hiding narcissism behind a show of good manners, Coward confesses, explores, teases the ruthlessness of his self-involvement. He lets laughter excuse it. In *Design for Living*, the unprincipled mischievousness of ambition, talent, and passion are on the surface of play instead of under it. Leo Mercure becomes a famous playwright. Otto Sylvus becomes a famous painter. Gilda, who shares their love and loves them both, is their equal in egotism. No Coward comedy is more intimately linked with the notion of stardom than *Design for Living*. Written as a star vehicle for himself and the Lunts, the play shows the tyranny of fame that allows stars to escape from normal attitudes and responsibilities.

'*Design for Living* as a project rather than as a play sat

patiently at the back of my mind for eleven years', Coward wrote. 'It had to wait until Lynn Fontanne, Alfred Lunt, and I had arrived, by different roads, at the exact moment in our careers when we felt that we could all three play together with a more or less equal degree of success.'[48] For success read fame. In *Present Indicative*, the issue of stardom is more clearly spelled out:

> From these shabby, congenial rooms, we projected ourselves into future eminence. We discussed, the three of us, over delicatessen potato salad and dill pickles, our most secret dreams of success. Lynn and Alfred were to be married. That was the first plan. Then they were to become definitely idols of the public. That was the second plan. Then, all this being successfully accomplished, they were to act exclusively together. This was the third plan. It remained for me to supply the fourth, which was that when all three of us had become stars of sufficient magnitude to be able to count upon an individual following irrespective of each other, then, poised serenely upon that enviable plane of achievement, we would meet and act triumphantly together . . .[49]

Design for Living is constructed on Coward's familiar symmetrical lines. In Act One, Gilda leaves Otto for Leo. In Act Two, she leaves Leo for Ernest, their mutual friend. In Act Three, she leaves Ernest to be reunited with Otto *and* Leo. This racy state of affaires was quick to be parodied. On Broadway in *Life Begins at 8:40* (1934), Louella Gear, Ray Bolger and Bert Lahr sang:

> Night and day, ma chérie
> Me for you, and you and you for me.
> We're living in the smart upper sets.
> Let other lovers sing their duets.
> Duets are made for the bourgeoisie – oh
> But only God can make a trio.

Although the play opens in a shabby Paris studio, the people who inhabit it live in a world of taste and accomplishment. Ernest Friedman's appearance at Otto's studio with a Matisse under his arm allows Coward immediately to juxtapose the ordinary with the extraordinary. As his name implies, Ernest is a conventional man, 'rather precise in manner', who responds to life in a fastidious way. As Gilda points out, Friedman, a picture dealer, is by nature a spectator whereas she and her two lovers do artistic things. They romanticize their selfishness as artistic impulse. 'I cannot, for the life of me, imagine why I'm so fond of you', Ernest tells Gilda. 'You have such abominable manners.' And she does. She exudes a bohemian indifference to any conventions. Gilda is an interior decorator. She has no ambitions to be a star, but all the self-centred attributes of one. Her conversation about the Matisse and Otto's painting serves to establish both her appeal and her amorality. As Gilda soon announces, she is restless and out of the ordinary. She longs for a setting to match her inflated self-esteem:

> GILDA (*she opens the window almost violently*): ... I'm sick of this studio!; it's squalid! I wish I were somewhere quite different. I wish I were a nice-minded British matron, with a husband, a cook, and a baby. I wish I believed in God and the *Daily Mail* and 'Mother India'!

All she apparently believes in is herself. 'Would you describe me as a super-egotist?' she asks Ernest, who concurs.

> GILDA: ... Thinking of myself too much, and not enough of other people?
> ERNEST: No. Thinking of other people too much through yourself.

Fame is the perversion of every man's need for validation and attention. Gilda's involvement with Leo and Otto provides her with the constant attention in private that they seek in public. She flaunts her egotism. She has 'no reverence', she dislikes women and their enchantments. She admits to something masculine and competitive in her nature: 'It humiliates me to the dust to think that I can go so far, clearly and intelligently, keeping faith with my own standards – which are not female standards at all – preserving a certain decent integrity, not using any tricks; then, suddenly, something happens, a spark is struck and down I go into the mud! Squirming with archness, being aloof and desirable, consciously alluring, snatching and grabbing, evading and surrendering, dressed and painted for victory ...' In love, her 'standards' prevent her from marrying. What Coward presents as an indication of Gilda's integrity is also a measure of her isolation – another aspect of a star's life she shares. Nothing ties her to society.

> GILDA: ... The only reason for me to marry would be these: to have children; to have a home; to have a background for social activities; and to be provided for. Well, I don't like children; I don't wish for a home; I can't bear social activities, and I have a small but adequate income of my own.

The ménage is another of Coward's private worlds, an elite with its own code of conduct. 'Look at us clearly as human beings', Gilda tells Ernest, 'rather peculiar human beings, I grant you, and don't be prejudiced by our lack of social grace.' To live beyond manners, beyond conventional definitions of normality requires a courage that Ernest doesn't have. 'Be brave', Gilda urges him. 'Look at the whole thing as a side show. People pay to see freaks. Walk up! Walk up and see the Fat Lady and the Monkey Man and the Living Skeleton and the Three Famous Hermaphrodites! – '.

Leo reiterates the myth of their extraordinary natures. Chaos is the price to be paid for such star-crossed allegiances. 'We all love each other a lot, far too much, and we've made a bloody mess of it! That was inevitable too.' But Leo proclaims them above the rules of society's game. Therefore, they are also above its accepted hypocrisies. 'If we were ordinary moral, high-thinking citizens,' Leo tells Gilda, who has a brief pang of conscience about Otto, 'we could carry on a backstairs affair for weeks without saying a word about it ...'. Star turns, they must live every triumph and tragedy out in the open. They must perform their passion for each other. Gilda and Leo are unrepentant about their pleasure. They relive the 'strong magic' of their previous gala evening and replay Leo's winning style. 'Your manner was a dream!', Gilda says. Leo's extra aura, his confidence and elan, is linked to his new success. 'Perhaps it's having money', Gilda says. 'Perhaps your success has given you a little extra glamour.' They have both been enchanted by each other's glamour.

When Otto returns, he finds Leo and Gilda laughing together. In due course, he is outraged. He first attacks them on grounds of bad manners ('Couldn't you have waited until I came back, and told me how you felt?'). Then Otto goes on to indict them, calling Leo 'a cheap, second-rate little opportunist ready to sacrifice anything to the excitement of the moment'. The Act ends with Otto spelling out Leo's success, and using his accomplishment as a sardonic blessing: 'Go ahead, my boy, and do great things! You've already achieved a Hôtel de Luxe, a few smart suits, and the woman I loved. Go ahead, maybe there are still higher peaks for you to climb. Good luck, both of you! Wonderful luck! I wish you were dead and in hell!' Having set all their egos in motion, Coward devotes Act Two to dramatizing their self-aggrandizement.

Coward, who had his first Rolls-Royce at 26 and his first biography at 33, knew what there was to know about stardom. Act Two begins with an image of Coward's alter-ego, Leo, galvanized by the new momentum of celebrity. He is reading his rave reviews. As the continual din of the telephone dramatizes, his name is not only triumphant but tyrannical. He is in constant, hectic demand. Parties, interviews, photographs, well-wishers – everyone wants part of his action. 'Success is far more perilous than failure, isn't it?' says Gilda who wants no part of the ballyhoo, nor is wanted by the nescafé society who clamour after Leo. She dismisses the people as 'second hand'. But the public attention is too alluring. Leo succumbs. He is happy to skim the surface of life. 'It's inevitable that the more successful I become, the

more people will run after me', he explains to Gilda. 'I don't
believe in their friendship, and I don't take them seriously,
but I enjoy them. Probably a damn sight more than they
enjoy me! I enjoy the whole damn thing. I've worked hard
for it all my life! They'll drop me, all right, when they're
tired of me.' Gilda puts the other side of the case: 'They
waste your time, these ridiculous celebrity-hunters, and they
sap your vitality'.

Coward managed to steer his career between the poles of
public adulation and hard work. But Leo and Gilda are
caught in the dilemma of celebrity which Coward 'solved' by
having a household organized around his eight o'clock to
one o'clock writing schedule; and live-in friends on call when
he wanted an audience or companionship. Companionship
is no longer the issue between Leo and Gilda. The world is
Leo's company; and, as Gilda later tells Otto, she is 'not
needed any more'. Leo offers marriage, but he's wedded
only to himself. The scene shows Leo's celebrity pulling him
away from Gilda, from their private world, from ordinary
decency. Having built a public self, Leo feels compelled to
pursue it. Leo and Gilda quarrel. Their past together is a
dead memory. Their future is only a destiny for one. 'With
the trumpets blowing and the flags flying and the telephone
ringing, we can still pretend', Gilda says, kicking at the
newspaper reviews on the floor as she exits. 'We can pretend
that we're happy.' Coward shows Leo trying to do just that:
putting a fine face over the phone only to let unhappiness
show through when a journalist from the *Evening Standard*
comes to interview him. In Coward's crude set-up, Leo
rounds on the oafish journalist. 'The whole business is grotesque. Don't you see how grotesque it is?' Even as he scolds
the press for hounding him, he craves the publicity. 'Call in
your photographer. Photograph me – and leave me alone.'
Gilda apologizes for the spat and goes off to shop. The
curtain comes down on the scene with Leo left smiling for
the camera.

The debate about celebrity continues in Scene 2 when

Otto pays Gilda an unexpected visit. The symmetry of Act One is reversed. Leo is away; and Otto returns transformed by *his* brand-new success. He is no sooner in the door than the conversation comes around to accomplishment:

> OTTO: New York. I had an exhibition there.
> GILDA: Was it successful?
> OTTO: Very, thank you.

Winners in a competitive society, stars of free enterprise, the famous are living embodiments of the society's economic rules. Gilda has no illusion about celebrity's vindictive triumph. 'The survival of the fittest – that's what counts', she tells Otto, echoing the star's credo. And Otto revels in the star's power to turn all life into capital:

> GILDA: You're so sure of yourself, aren't you? You're both so sure of yourselves, you and Leo. Getting what you want must be terribly gratifying!
> OTTO (*unruffled*): It is.

In this world of unfettered self-involvement, Otto and Gilda talk charmingly, endlessly, about themselves and their triangle. They toast their passion ('Perhaps not love, exactly' says Gilda. 'Something a little below it and a little above it, but something terribly strong'). And in this replay of Leo's love scene in Act One, Otto is allowed to crow about being above the standards of society.

> GILDA: The whole thing's degrading, completely and utterly degrading.
> OTTO. Only when measured up against other people's standards ... We are different. Our lives are diametrically opposed to ordinary social conventions; and it's no use grabbing at those conventions to hold us up when we find ourselves in deep water. We've jilted them and eliminated them, and we've got to find our own solutions for our own peculiar moral problems.

In the end, buoyed by Coward's coy words of passion ('I want to make love to you very badly indeed, please!'), the triangle tips momentarily in Otto's direction.

Scene 3 allows Gilda *her* moment of self-aggrandizement. Armed with the sure knowledge of the Darwinian struggle ('The survival of the fittest, that's the light', she tells Ernest), Gilda leaves twin 'dear John' notes for Otto and Leo. Like her lovers, she sets off to exploit – what else? – her true unboundaried self:

GILDA: ... In the future I intend to be only one thing.
ERNEST. That being – ?
GILDA. Myself, Ernest. My unadulterated self! Myself, without hangings, without trimmings, unencumbered by the winding tendrils of other people's demands –

When Leo and Otto discover they have been jilted, they start to drink. 'Gilda doesn't care for successful people', Leo says. And Otto, echoing his curtain lines in Act One, says with sudden fury: '... Good luck to her I say. Good luck to the old girl – she knows her onions'. They toast their immortal souls. The irony of their soullessness seems to be lost on Coward who makes their sodden cameraderie charming. They vow to revel in success. Coward himself admitted much the same: 'I am determined to travel through life first-class'.[50] And Leo puts the same case for making fame's greed glorious. 'Let's make the most of the whole business, shall we?' Leo coaxes Otto:

Let's be photographed and interviewed and pointed at in restaurants! Let's play the game for all it's worth, secretaries and fur coats and *de luxe* suites on transatlantic liners at minimum rates! Don't let's allow one shabby perquisite to slip through our fingers! It's what we dreamed many years ago and now it's within our reach. Let's cash in, Otto, and see how much we lose by it ... Success in twenty lessons! Each one more bitter than the last! More and better Success! Louder and funnier Success!

Leo's design for living without Gilda is a star's familiar vindictive triumph. Leo and Otto will get even for private rejection by flaunting their public success. They make their Faustian bargain and are prepared to be trivialized by it. Leo gives the speech with 'a glint in his eye' that makes his immodest proposal seem a fine adventure. But fame is a neurotic defence that dramatizes vindictiveness as drive, megalomania as commitment, hysteria as action, greed as just reward. Behind Leo's and Otto's comic selfishness are destructive assumptions that Coward can't and won't pursue. Instead, he works another comic twist by making Leo and Otto the new couple. The curtain falls on Act Two with them in a teary, drunken embrace:

> OTTO: Thank God for each other, anyhow!
> LEO: That's true. We'll get along, somehow – (*his voice breaks*) – together –
> OTTO (*struggling with his tears*): Together –
> LEO (*giving way to his, and breaking down completely*): But we're going to be awfully – awfully lonely –
> *They both sob hopelessly on each other's shoulders.*

In Act Three, Gilda too has ended up in hog heaven. Sealed away from the struggle for survival in a New York penthouse, Gilda is surrounded by fine things and swank people. She has married Ernest, the man whose personality she'd defended so haughtily in Act One.

> OTTO: Ernest hasn't got a personality.
> GILDA: Yes, he has: but only a little one, gentle and prim.

Everything in Gilda's house, except Ernest's paintings, is for sale. The implication is that Gilda herself has gone to the highest bidder. The price she's had to pay for stability is the lowered amperage of her artistic personality. 'Her manner has changed a good deal. She is much more still and sure than before', Coward's stage directions read. 'A certain amount of vitality has gone from her, but, in its place, there is an aloof poise quite in keeping with her dress and surroundings.' Her manner is meant to be as perfect as her surroundings.

When Leo and Otto enter Gilda's world – themselves seeming models of perfection 'attired in very faultless evening dress' – they bring their disruptive energy to the studied order of the place. 'Artistically too careful, but professionally superb', is Otto's shrewd judgement of the decor. These votaries of passion, who respect nothing but their own gratification, confound the other guests by their outrageous behaviour. They have come to pull Gilda back into their orbit, away from propriety and back into turmoil. 'Life is a pleasure trip', Leo tells one of stodgy guests, 'a Cheap Excursion'. With their vicious put-ons and put-downs, Leo and Otto are a double-act of disenchantment. Their performance is for their own amusement. They don't listen, sympathize, or care about anyone but Gilda. They want to return to their exclusive isolation. Their bad manners are a way of clearing the room. 'They wouldn't go – they were going to stay for ever and ever!' Leo says in a quick, whispered explanation of their bad behaviour at the end of the scene. Leo and Otto are quick to remind Gilda of the passion and the danger they represent. 'How far have you grown away, my dear love?' Leo says to her. 'How lonely are you in your little box so high above the arena? Don't you ever feel that you want to come down in the cheap seats again, nearer to the blood and the sand and the warm smells, nearer to Life and Death.' Leo and Otto are Coward's metaphor of the predatory, volatile nature of sexuality which he translates into a battle of manners. Gilda struggles to maintain her social poise and fends off their tempestuousness. 'Laughing lightly' she coaxes Otto to 'behave yourself'. As their sarcasm gets nearer the knuckle, Gilda tells the guests 'they both talk the most absurd nonsense' and warns them to pay no attention. Manners impose a carapace of normality on craving. Otto and Leo know Gilda's secret heart and what her 'good manners' hide. Their verbal fencing has a dangerous undertone.

81

OTTO: Don't undermine our social poise, Gilda, you – who have so much!

GILDA (*sharply*): Your social poise is non-existent.

LEO: We have a veneer, though; it's taken us years to acquire; don't scratch it with your sharp witty nails – *darling*!

Everybody jumps slightly at the word 'darling'.

Manners are starting to break down; and Coward intends the cracks in the facade to be seen. The dialogue insists on it.

GILDA (*laughing a trifle wildly*): Stop it both of you! You're behaving abominably!

OTTO: We're all behaving abominably.

LEO: The veneer is wearing thin. Even yours, Gilda.

Gilda plays up but gives the game away when she 'winks violently at them' and slips them the house key while ushering all her guests including them out of the house. Their old intimacy has not been lost, only forestalled. Coward ends the scene with a stage picture of Gilda's agitation. She paces the room, then bolts for the firescape. The audience is left wondering how the romantic equation will factor out at the finale.

In Coward's antic version of love conquers all, Gilda decides to live with both Leo and Otto. The homosexual daydream of sexual abundance comes true. Ernest is quickly and brazenly sidestepped. His indignation at the cruelty of their behaviour only confirms the unfairness of the comic world, in which every outrage is redeemed by laughter. Everything Ernest says about Leo and Otto is true. They are ruthless, arrogant, egotistical and defiantly unreasonable. But Gilda opts for the excitement and danger of their passion.

ERNEST: You're – you're insane! You can't be serious.

GILDA: I'm not serious! That's what's so dreadful. I feel I ought to be, but I'm not – my heart's bobbing up and down inside me like a parrot in a cage! It's shameful, I know, but I can't help it – ...

Frivolity reasserts itself at the moment of crisis. The tone is the triumph of ego over what it sees as sterile experience. There are no standards, no boundaries, no conventions which bind the trio to society except their own sensational selfishness. 'From now on we shall have to live and die our own way', Gilda says, sounding the clarion call of the talentocracy. 'No one else's way is any good, we don't fit.' Unlike her interior decorating business which she's prepared to give up without batting an eyelid, the menage is not a vocation but a destiny. The threesome reunite and banish the figure of normality. In their triumvirate of talent, Ernest has always been the odd man out, always 'little Ernest'. He is the businessman, the dealer, the voyeur, someone who lives on the outskirts of the bohemian world untouched by the delirium of talent. The trio disdain him and cast him out.

ERNEST: You're a mad woman again.
GILDA: Why shouldn't I be a mad woman? I've been sane and still for two years. You were deceived by my dead behaviour because you wanted to be ...

Gilda has a star's craving for action; and the menage has all the daring visibility of a star turn. The whole purpose of being sensational is to call attention to yourself. Gilda, like her lovers, shares the vulgar ambition for attention. Notoriety confirms her sense of being extraordinary. Otto tells Ernest, 'She could never be happy without a fuss. She revels in it'.

Coward's comic revenge at the finale is the victory of the disguised gay world over the straight one. Coward uses Ernest as the puppet of the straight world which the trio persistently slap down. The man who calls them 'degenerates' literally falls on his face. Ernest berates their 'false and distorted values', their lack of decency. 'We have our own decencies', says Coward's spokesman, Leo, coming on strong at the curtain. 'We have our own ethics. Our lives are a different shape from yours. Wave us good-bye, Little

Ernest, we're together again'. Ernest continues to work himself into a fury over their 'disgusting three-sided erotic
hotch-potch!.' He vilifies their taste. Otto retorts, 'Certain
emotions transcend even taste'. He screams at them to be
quiet. Leo crows back at him, 'Why should we be quiet? ...
Why should you have a monopoly on noise? Why should
your pompous moral pretensions be allowed to hurtle across
this city without any competition? We've all got lungs; let's
use them! Let's shriek like mad! Let's enjoy ourselves!'

Leo's call for liberation (which echoes *The Young Idea*) is
what triumphs at the finale. Ernest hasn't the charm or the
wit to outpoint them in this prize fight. The gravity of
Ernest's charges about their 'shifty', 'irresponsible', and
'abominable' behaviour does not touch them. But the trio's
flippancy drives Ernest crazy. It implies a meaninglessness
which threatens all the aspirations and values by which he
lives. Ernest storms out of the room and trips over some
paintings. The trio begins to laugh, and Coward means this
equivocal laughter to assume the resonance of symbol. 'They
groan and weep with laughter; their laughter is still echoing
from the walls as – the curtain falls.'

'Different minds found different meanings in this laughter', Coward wrote later, slightly fudging the issue. 'Some
considered it to be directed against Ernest, Gilda's husband
and the time-honoured friend of all three. If so, it was
certainly cruel, and in the worst possible taste. Some saw in
it the lascivious anticipation of some carnal frolic. Others,
with less ribald imaginations, regarded it as a meaningless
and slightly inept excuse to bring the curtain down. I as the
author, however, prefer to think that Gilda and Otto and
Leo were laughing at themselves.'[51]

Coward's laughter is the theatrical equivalent of tiptoeing
away from chaos. The trio escape the consequences of their
actions. The laughter binds the talentocracy together, beyond good manners and conventional morals. (The mythic
photo of Coward and the Lunts clutching each other's hands
as they laugh, their bodies draped across each other in an

impermeable triangle makes the point.) Their laughter is self-congratulatory and victorious. It is the final image of frivolity which rules over the bad manners, in Coward's best work.

'I love high comedy', Coward said. 'A lot can be said in terms of it.'[52] In *Design for Living* Coward tried to say too much. 'I don't like propaganda', he said, 'unless it's disguised so brilliantly that it is entertainment.'[53] While he succeeded in providing the Lunts and himself with an actors' lark, Coward failed to find a proper metaphor for his ideas. The issue of abnormal sexuality and success are never fully integrated into the action of the play the way role-playing is into *Hay Fever* or charm into *Present Laughter* or frivolity into *Private Lives*. *Design for Living* is strangely off-kilter. Still, Coward considered it among his best efforts. 'To quote Madame Arcati, "It came to me in a blinding flash",' Coward wrote in 1958, recounting how sometimes he taxed himself for being a foolish, superficial, capering lightweight. 'I had written several important plays – *Hay Fever*, *Private Lives*, *Design for Living*, *Present Laughter* and *Blithe Spirit* ... They mirrored, without over-exaggeration, a certain section of the social life of the times and, on re-reading them, I find them both unpretentious and well-constructed.'[54]

Design for Living, written in 1932, was performed to great acclaim in New York in 1933; but because of the Lord Chamberlain's objections had to wait until 1939 for its English debut. The show ran 203 performances before the outbreak of war interrupted the run. In this climate of re-newed national mission and peril, Coward's daring frivolity now looked like the end of an era. 'The kind of smartly silly bantering which goes on in this play, especially in the first scene of Act Three, is very much of its time and already seems a trifle faded', wrote the *Observer*. 'It will not be long before they revive it in costume as a specimen of the "early thirties" manners – or a hangover from the twittering twenties.'[55]

85

Design for Living fails because it is too contrived. The play's belaboured sensationalism finally makes the trio's bad manners both unsurprising and unmoving. But Coward's one-act romp *Hands Across the Sea* (1936), another chronicle of a charmed and closed circle of friends, is a brilliant piece of social reporting in which the outrageousness of egocentricity is completely believable and therefore theatrically astonishing. Sir Terence Rattigan called the play 'just about the best short comedy ever written'.[56] It shows Coward at his most impish. Unlike *Hay Fever* where the guests don't know the rules or *Private Lives* and *Design for Living* where the characters play by their own rules, everyone who attends the upper-class gathering hastily assembled by the Gilpins to repay the Rawlingsons from Malaya for their hospitality, knows the rules. But knowing the rules of the social game is no longer enough. You have to be asked to play. The Gilpins' indifference to the Wadhursts whom they mistake as the Rawlingsons, as well as Mr. Burnham, a messenger with speedboat designs for Commander Gilpin, is breathtaking. 'By some magic', Rattigan writes, '[the author's flight of fancy] persuades us that the only unreal elements are the sad, dreadfully sane couple from Malaya, crouching timidly in a corner, and watching the goings-on with wide, wondering eyes. Them we instantly reject as "things from another world". Everything else – the duck that quacks 'Land of Hope and Glory' when its behind is pinched, the Maharajah who may or may not have a religious objection to Douglas Byng, the son of a lunatic mother who did something unspeakable in Hong Kong because of the climate – all this we accept as substantial, tangible, true and of this world.'[57]

The play testifies to Coward's genius for mimicry. 'Lord Louis and Lady Louis Mountbatten used to give cocktail parties and people used to arrive that nobody ever heard of and sit about and go away again', Coward recalled about the genesis of the play. 'Somebody Dickie had met somewhere, or somebody Edwina had met – and nobody knew who they were. We all talked among ourselves.'[58] Coward's

The Sketch

Registered as a Newspaper for Transmission in the United Kingdom and to Canada and Newfoundland by Magazine Post.

No. 1683—Vol. CXXX.   WEDNESDAY, APRIL 29, 1925.   ONE SHILLING.

NOEL THE FORTUNATE : THE YOUNG PLAYWRIGHT, ACTOR, AND COMPOSER, MR. NOEL COWARD, BUSY AT BREAKFAST.

Noel Coward is probably the most famous man of his age in England, as he is but twenty-five, and is the author of two plays now running in town—"The Vortex" and "Fallen Angels"—has written the book, lyrics, and some of the music for the new Charles B. Cochran revue, "On with the Dance," which is due at the London Pavilion on April 30, and is leading man in the cast of his much-praised and constantly discussed "The Vortex." As our photograph shows, Mr. Noel Coward begins to get busy at breakfast !

Photograph by Stage Photo. Co.

3

4

send up of Lord Louis Mountbatten, who was then in the Admiralty, didn't strike the family as funny. 'It was a bare-faced parody of our lives, with Gertie playing Lady Maureen Gilpin and Noël Coward playing me', Lord Mountbatten said, recalling being sent six free tickets when *Tonight at 8:30* opened, in which *Hands Across the Sea* featured. 'Absolutely outrageous and certainly not worth six free tickets!'[59] Having adopted an upper-middle-class stance, Coward was a master at impersonating both its manners and its sound. The fluting lunacy of the Gilpins' banter zeroes in on the self-involvement of a class in which everyone is treated as an extra in their epic.

The joke in all Coward's other major comedies is the central characters' staggering impoliteness, which they somehow manage to get away with. In *Hands Across the Sea*, the situation is reversed. The Gilpins want to be polite; but their instincts for generosity have been atrophied by selfishness. From the outset of the play, 'Piggie' and 'Peter' Gilpin are vague about the Rawlingsons whose name 'Piggie' sees on the telephone pad and whom she realizes have been invited to the house.

PIGGIE: ... My God!
PETER: What is it?
PIGGIE: The Rawlingsons.
PETER: Who the hell are they?
PIGGIE: I'd forgotten all about them.

'Piggie' wants to repay hospitality; but her instincts for the right social response are more acute than her ability to respond to people. She spends anxious minutes on the phone trying to hustle up a social agenda. 'Mother and father and daughter', she tells Maud, the first of many disembodied characters at the other end of the phone. 'You must remember – pretty girl with bad legs – No – they didn't have a son – we swore we'd give them a lovely time when they came home on leave – I know they didn't have a son, that was those other people in Penang.'

In the pauses and detours of the conversation, Maud's questions, her personality, her turn of mind are apparent without ever being seen. While 'Piggie' rushes off to change, the Gilpins' entourage as well as the strangers enter. The Wadhursts have also been invited to the Gilpin house and been forgotten about. The stage directions characterize the Wadhursts as 'timid' and Mr. Burnham as 'non-descript'. They sink into the background as the voluble old friends and the din of telephone conversations take over.

The telephone dominates the party, at once a symbol of the connections and the isolation of the Gilpins. The old Gilpin friends swoop down on the receiver to hoot and holler about their lives. Occasionally, social conversation spills over into the telephone conversation, and then back again. The effect is dreamlike and surreal:

PIGGIE: How much do torpedoes cost each?
BOGEY: What? – (*at telephone*) – wait a minute, Piggie's yelling at me –
PIGGIE: Torpedoes – (*She makes a descriptive gesture.*)
BOGEY: Oh, thousands and thousands – terribly expensive things – ask Peter – (*at telephone*) – If I do bring him you'll have to be frightfully nice to him . . .

Sometimes the telephone-talkers break off to announce bits of gossip or get unlikely information to feed to the invisible person at the other end of the line. In the process a whole cast of unseen characters and their world of privilege comes to life: Laura Mersham wrestling with a Maharajah all the way to Newmarket on the front seat of his car; Nina's 'Indian ding-dong', Vera's scene with Lady Borrowdale, Freda Brathurst's naughty son, Boodie's return. The room resounds with talk of these people and their antics. They are real but unseen, while the Wadhursts and Mr. Burnham remain seen but unreal. Although the telephone conversations are obviously monologues, Coward writes them with such panache that they seem to be duologues. By repeating the improbable incidents in various phone calls, the incredible becomes ordinary. The problems of entertaining Maharajahs are spun out and brought together when 'Piggie' takes the phone, agreeing to go to Nina's party if her friend Clare will go.

> PIGGIE (*at telephone*): She's moaning a bit, but I'll persuade her – what happens after dinner? – the man with the duck from the Café de Paris – (*to the room in general*). She's got that sweet duck from the Café de Paris – ... But, darling, do you think it quite *wise* – I mean Maharajas are terribly touchy and there's probably something in their religion about ducks being mortal sin or something – you know how difficult they are about cows and pigs – just a minute (*To the Wadhursts*) You can tell us, of course –
> MRS. WADHURST: I beg your pardon?
> PIGGIE: Do Indians mind ducks?
> MRS. WADHURST: I – I don't think so – ...

While the telephone is passed like a baton between 'Piggie' and her friends, she tries to chat up the Wadhursts whom she assumes are the Rawlingsons. She is all poise and no empathy. Caught up in her social performance, 'Piggie' can't imagine the Wadhursts' social nervousness or their suffering. She doesn't really hear them or see them. A resplendently high-camp creation, 'Piggie', as her name implies, is both a hilarious comic turn and Coward's unspoken indictment of the evils of a class.

> PIGGIE (*to Mrs. Wadhurst*): How's your daughter?
> MRS. WADHURST (*surprised*): She's a little better, thank you.
> PIGGIE: Oh, has she been ill? I'm so sorry.
> MRS. WADHURST (*gently*): She's been ill for five years.
> PIGGIE (*puzzled*): How dreadful for you – are you happy with that cocktail, or would you rather have tea?

Friends clamber over the furniture and the Wadhursts to get to the phone. 'Excuse me', says Clare, getting past Mrs. Wadhurst and taking the receiver. She talks into it: 'Darling – I'm dead with surprise – ' The hilarious line also underscores the irony of the situation. To all intents and purposes the Wadhursts are not living. Their actual identities are unacknowledged. 'Piggie' can make no real contact with them. When the phone rings and the voice at the other end announces 'Mrs. Rawlingson', 'Piggie' thinks it's a request and hands the receiver to Mrs. Wadhurst who flounders a second and then hands it back to 'Piggie'. Mrs. Rawlingson is calling to beg off from the party. 'Piggie' hangs up 'slowly ... looking at the Wadhursts in complete bewilderment'. 'That was Mrs. Rawlingson', 'Piggie' says – 'brightly, but with intense meaning'.

The play edges toward farce as Peter goes to the piano and begins to hum a tune to his wife.

> PETER (*humming to a waltz refrain, slightly indistinctly but clearly enough for PIGGIE to hear*): If these are not them who are they? Who are they? Who are they?
> *PIGGIE rises and saunters over to the piano.*
> PIGGIE: Play the other bit, dear, out of the second act – (*She hums*) – you know – 'I haven't the faintest idea – Oh no – I haven't the faintest idea'.
> PETER (*changing tempo*): 'Under the light of the moon, dear – you'd better find out pretty soon, dear.'

When 'Piggie' finally figures out the Wadhursts' identity, they're on their feet and nearly out the door. A whole whirlwind has taken place around them, and they have neither touched nor been touched by it. After they've gone, their spectral presence is reinforced by 'Piggie's' memory of them:

> PIGGIE: Wasn't it frightful – poor angels – I must ring up Maud – (*She dials a number*) – I think they had a heavenly time though, don't you – I mean they couldn't have noticed a thing –

It's 'Piggie' and her yapping friends who've noticed nothing. 'Piggie' doesn't even see Mr. Burnham who huddles in a corner waiting for the right moment to announce himself and deliver the plans for Peter's speedboat. When she rushes out to get nail varnish to do her toes, Burnham nervously explains his mission to Clare. 'You should have piped up before', she tells him preparing to leave the party. Mr. Burnham, the stage direction reads, 'retires again into the shadows'.

'The trouble with Maud is, she's too insular,' says 'Piggie' as she settles back on the sofa painting her toes. Even as she picks up the phone to speak with yet another of her pedigreed friends ('No, I'm quite alone doing my feet . . .'), Mr. Burnham tiptoes out of the room. The familiar, ghostly Coward comedy exit is interrupted by 'Piggie' who 'catches sight of him just as he is gingerly opening the door'. Coward builds the play to this moment and then effortlessly rings one last bad-mannered twist out of the plot. 'Oh, good-bye', says 'Piggie'. 'It's been absolutely lovely, you're the sweetest family I've ever met in my life'. Mr. Burnham has been noticed, but he remains unseen. 'Piggie's' show of 'good manners' exposes her moral and intellectual slovenliness. In Coward's satire, 'Piggie's' outrageousness elevates myopia to myth. She becomes a high-camp emblem of her class, insisting on politeness and quietly doing violence while under the impression she is displaying good form.

3

'Savonarola in Evening Dress'?

'I have never felt the necessity of being "with it". I'm all for staying in my place.'

Noël Coward

Even when they have no political convictions, stars serve a political function. Multi-national corporations of one, stars are proof that capitalism works. They are figures of hope whose gifts create an illusory optimism for the public who always pays well for forgetfulness. 'My word, what good fun they gave us', wrote Janet Flanner of the Coward–Lawrence partnership in the thirties. 'How secure they made our theatrical pleasure'.[1]

Coward confidently dominated the stage world while the real world of pre-war England was in turmoil. Coward seemed to be everywhere. 'I was writing plays, acting plays, directing plays, writing lyrics, composing music, making gramophone records, broadcasting and travelling', he wrote in *Future Indefinite*, his second volume of autobiography. 'I was a highly publicized, irritatingly successful figure and much in demand.'[2]

Coward's influence was magnified by the emergence of records and radio which allowed songs to make his presence and his 'pessimism with pep' more widely felt. Coward understood the potency of cheap music. So did the Government. When England went to war, the Government not only vetted lyrics played to the troops but sent Coward himself to far-flung theatres of battle to perform his beloved satirical repertoire. Coward was not as sure-footed in the political arena as he was in comedy. Coward's displays of political sentiment – *Post-Mortem* (1930), *Cavalcade* (1931), *This*

Happy Breed (written 1939, staged 1942), *Peace in Our Time* (1947) – were almost always the triumph of technique over temperament.

'Dear boy', Coward told the New York *Times* correspondent while being interviewed on his seventieth birthday. 'I've had no social causes. Do I have to? I wanted to write good plays, to grip as well as amuse . . . No I have no great social causes. I can't think of any off-hand. If I did, they'd be very off-hand.'[3] And so they were. Dubbed a 'Savonarola in evening dress',[4] Coward saved his mischievous satire for the manners of a class. He was not a hater, but a celebrator. In the twenties, he typified the era's political apathy. In no revue sketch, no song, no play of that decade does Coward make any direct reference to current events.[5] Coward lived at a long arm's length from the lower middle class he lionized in *This Happy Breed*. A self-confessed 'celebrity snob',[6] he valued 'people of achievement';[7] and the ordinary folk Coward wrote into *Cavalcade*, *This Happy Breed*, *Peace in Our Time* and the film *In Which We Serve* (1942) suffer from the imaginative distance he put between them and himself. Coward was riding too high to take more than a passing interest in the upheavals of the English lower classes. He was untouched by the Depression. 'THE WORLD'S RICHEST WRITERS', headlined the *Sunday Daily Express* in 1932, 'Coward 1; GBS 2; A. A. Milne 3'.[8] The paper reported that since 1929 Coward's annual income was £50,000.

Wealth bred a certain *richesse oblige* in him. 'If I don't care for things', Coward said, epitomizing the blinkered optimism of boulevard theatre, 'I simply don't look at them'.[9] This was not an attitude that asked hard questions of English life or yielded hard answers. He was rich and famous from poking fun at English manners. But England made him; and his love for his country was as rock solid as his public persona. The thought of sending up England 'would shock me to the core', he told the BBC, 'I'd never dream of doing so'.[10] Even political messages on stage sent the wind up Coward. He liked to tell the story of going to

93

the theatre with an actress who said, 'If it's a play with a message, I shan't dress'.[11]

'I am inclined to wager that the sweet and not the bitter life is Mr. Coward's forte', wrote James Agate about Coward's first attempt at a protest play, *Post-Mortem*. It was a safe bet. *Post-Mortem* was intended as a knock-out punch but ended up as a flabby jab at the futility of war and the press barons who fanned the flames of militarism. It never had a professional production. The play was composed on a voyage home from Singapore where Coward had performed in a production of R.C. Sherriff's *Journey's End* and was still full of emotion about the failure of World War 1 to win a better world. (Coward was more successful at parodying *Journey's End* than matching it. In *Words and Music* (1932), the sketch 'Journey's End' camps up carnage, with actors shooting puffs of powder out of diamanté rifles; balloons being flung onto the stage from the pit and boxes; the orchestra playing 'Deutschland über Alles'; and, representing the German and British, the chorus jumping over barbed wire, 'leaping gaily and pelting each other with coloured paper-streamers'.)

Coward begins and ends *Post-Mortem* at the Front Line in 1917. 'Somebody must be learning something from all this', says John Craven, the idealistic son of an English press baron, and the voice of optimism that Coward pits against the cynicism of his fellow soldier Perry Lomas who believes society will learn nothing from the carnage. 'They'll slip back into their smug illusions', Lomas tells Craven, 'England will make it hot for them if they don't'. When Craven is mortally wounded on night patrol, his spirit time-travels forward to 1930 to see if he or Lomas is right. He visits his mother, his former fiancée, his father in Fleet Street – and Perry, whose novel about war is being pilloried and who commits suicide. At the finale, Craven expires on the battlefield with the play's last words: 'You were right, Perry – a poor joke.'

The frivolity in Coward's comedies vivifies the sense of profound disillusion that is still-born in *Post-Mortem*. In *Post-Mortem*, Coward tries to overwhelm the audience with intensity. 'I wrote it from too hot off the grid', Coward told the BBC.[12] As Coward well understood, *Post-Mortem* suffered from a lack of detachment. 'I passionately believed in the truth of what I was writing; too passionately. The truths I snarled out in that hot, uncomfortable little cabin were all too true and mostly too shallow. Through lack of detachment and lack of real experience of my subject, I muddled the issues of the play.'[13]

In the following speech, which Coward wrongly admired 'as some of the best writing I have ever done,'[14] Lomas gives Coward's first 'State of England' speech. His rhythmless generalizations have more impact than sense. But in 1930, Coward had the prescience to imagine that the 'war to end all wars' would not be England's last battle:

Nothing's happening, really [Perry tells John when he returns in 1930]. There are strides being made forward in science and equal sized strides being made backwards in hypocrisy. People are just the same, individually pleasant and collectively idiotic. Machinery is growing magnificently, people paint pictures of it and compose ballets about it, the artists are cottoning on to that very quickly because they're scared that soon there won't be any other sort of beauty left, and they'll be stranded with nothing to paint, and nothing to write ... Politically, all is confusion, but that's nothing new. There's still poverty, unemployment, pain, greed, cruelty, passion and crime ... The competitive sporting spirit is being admirably fostered, particularly as regards the Olympic games. A superb preparation for the next War, fully realized by everyone but the public that will be involved. The newspapers still lie over anything of importance, and the majority still believes them implicitly. The only real difference in Post War conditions is that there are so many men maimed for life and still existing, and so many women whose heartache will never heal. The rest is the same only faster, and more meretricious ... It's all a joke with nobody to laugh at it ...

In *Cavalcade* Coward found a sensational theatrical method for detaching history from cynicism, politics from human suffering. He turned them into spectacle. *Cavalcade* was Coward's brilliant mass-manoeuvre. Coward showed the highlights of English history from New Year's Eve 1899 to New Year's Eve 1930 in 22 terse scenes and with a cast of 250. Size became content; Coward's technical accomplishment disarmed criticism. In skating on thin ice, one's safety is in speed; and momentum was crucial to Coward's concept. 'Noël knew he wanted something like Pageant or Procession', writes Cole Lesley in *The Life of Noël Coward*. 'He finally shouted "Cavalcade! A procession on horseback".'[15] Coward was the performing workhorse. He wrote, directed and composed the music for *Cavalcade*, whose finale was the superb 'Twentieth Century Blues'.

'I'm doing a very fancy production at the Drury Lane in September', Coward wrote to T. E. Lawrence. 'If you want to see *real* wheels going round let me know.'[16] The idea for *Cavalcade* had come to him while thumbing through an old issue of *Illustrated London News*. *Cavalcade* was a kind of illustrated history which spoke as strongly in its stage pictures and nostalgic songs as it did in dialogue. *Cavalcade* fitted Coward's urge, confided to his producer C. B. Cochran in 1930, 'to test my producing powers on a large scale'.[17] So much for political commitment.

Cavalcade opened on 13 October 1931. Three weeks before, on 21 September, England went off the gold standard, an event that sent unwarranted panic through the society and proved to be a turning point. 'This was the end of an age', A. J. P. Taylor wrote of the abandonment of the gold standard. 'Until 21 September 1931, men were hoping some how to restore the self-operating economy which had existed, or was supposed to have existed, before 1914. After that day, they had to face conscious direction at any rate so far as money was concerned.'[18]

Cavalcade seemed to encapsulate both the nostalgia and the foreboding of the moment. The spectacle revelled in the grandeur and sacrifices of the English, leading up to 1930 and a vision of 'CHAOS'. With its tableaux of Queen Victoria's death, the delights of the Edwardian music hall and high life, Mafeking Night, the outbreak of war, cheering the Armistice, the show tapped deep reservoirs of public feeling, the profound nostalgia for a world irretrievably lost. The contemporary bewilderment which Coward's stagecraft made spectacular at the play's finale had already arrived:

> ... across the darkness runs a Riley light sign spelling out news. Noise grows louder and louder. Steam rivets, loud speakers, jazz bands, aeroplane propellers, etc., until the general effect is complete chaos.

Coward's faith in duty, courage and country came brazenly through at the climax. A messenger of hope, Coward had few finer moments. His stage directions deftly transformed a poetic vision of chaos into a grand-slam image of lyrical patriotism:

> ... Suddenly it all fades into darkness and silence and away at the back a Union Jack glows through the blackness.
>
> The lights slowly come up and the whole stage is composed of massive tiers, upon which stand the entire Company. The Union Jack flies over their heads as they sing 'God Save the King'.
>
> THE END

Two weeks after the opening the Conservatives swept into power; and Coward was congratulated for his political savvy in choosing the right moment to mount his spectacle. 'Here', he wrote, 'I must regretfully admit that during rehearsals I was so very much occupied in the theatre, and, as usual, so bleakly uninterested in politics, that I had not the remotest idea, until a few days before production, that there was going to be a general election at all! However, there was, and its effects on the box office were considerable.'[19]

Whatever Coward's disclaimers about his political intuitions, when he was called onto the Drury Lane stage on opening night, Coward caught the wave of patriotic fervour and rode it straight to the bank. 'I hope that this play made you feel that, in spite of the troublous times we are living in, it is still pretty exciting to be English.'[20] The 'violent outburst of cheering'[21] (it lasted five minutes) that greeted Coward's words was matched the next day by the critical response of the press. The headlines said it all: 'GENIUS' (*Morning Post*); 'WONDER SHOW at Drury Lane' (*Daily Mirror*); 'CAVALCADE A GREAT PAGEANT' (*News Chronicle*); 'A STUPENDOUS CAVALCADE: Noël Coward Devises Drury Lane's Greatest Drama: Vast Crowds in Amazing Stage Pictures' (*Evening Standard*).

The political impact of *Cavalcade* mushroomed with current events, and caught Coward by surprise. 'Everybody seemed to be more concerned with *Cavalcade* as a patriotic appeal than as a play', he wrote. 'This attitude I realized had been enhanced by my first-night speech ... I rather wished I hadn't said it, hadn't popped it on to the top of *Cavalcade* like a paper hat.'[22] Even without his curtain speech, *Cavalcade*'s final champagne toast was a gallant rhetorical flourish calculated to tug at every English heartstring: '... let's drink to the hope that one day this country of ours, which we love so much, will find dignity and greatness and peace again'.

Cavalcade's instincts were commercial, not political. But Coward's success with the middle classes reinforced the idea that what was good for the middle classes was good for the country as a whole. The play served as a symbol of social integration. Two weeks into the run, the King, Queen, and entire Royal Family attended *Cavalcade*, a gesture, guessed *The Post*, 'meant to show his [the King's] people that their resolve and purpose had been understood ...'[23] The King's appearance at the play was front page news: 'THE KING SEES CAVALCADE: Great Outbursts of Loyalty: National Anthem Fervour';[24] 'THE KING'S GREAT OVATION AT CAVALCADE: Cheered for 5 Minutes: Enthusiasm in the Streets: Police Cordon Broken'.[25]

Not since Armistice Night, perhaps not since Mafeking Night [wrote the *Daily Telegraph*] has there been such a tumultuous demonstration of loyalty. Thousands of people surged around the theatre, and the appearance of the King, followed by the Queen and other members of the Royal Family, was the signal for a demonstration that will be historic.

All the pent-up emotions of a sorely tried nation – joy and relief that a crisis had been faced and passed . . .

Fifty years on, Coward's story and his grasp of history seem thin. Even then, rumours circulated that *Cavalcade* was 'begun, though not completed, tongue in cheek'.[26] *Cavalcade* shows off Coward's skill as a storyteller. The undeniable impact of the piece comes not from Coward's famed wit or from memorable characters, but from his substantial powers of organization. His history lesson has an irresistible symmetry.

Coward takes two families – the upper-class Marryots and the lower-class Bridges and follows the changing fortunes of masters and servants through the shifts of three decades. The symmetry which is hidden in Coward's comedies becomes a showy, comforting part of Coward's historical mosaic. Although the lives of the Marryots and the Bridges move along different vectors, they eventually intersect when the Marryots' youngest boy, Joe, falls in love with Fanny Bridges who has become an actress and moved up the social ladder. As the Marryots' world shrinks ('We've both outstayed our welcome' says Jane Marryot to her husband as they prepare to see in the new decade of the thirties), the Bridges' world expands. Coward makes the point bluntly when Jane Marryot and Ellen Bridges meet to discuss their children's future (II, 10). Ellen is now aggressive; and Jane's voice is tinged with bitterness.

> ELLEN: I suppose you imagine my daughter isn't good enough to marry your son . . . Fanny's received everywhere; she knows all the best people.
> JANE: How nice for her; I wish I did.

ELLEN: Things aren't what they used to be, you know – it's all changing.

JANE: Yes, I see it is.

ELLEN: Fanny's at the top of the tree now; she's having the most wonderful offers.

But theatrical spectacle wants to display life, not debate it. Coward pulls the scene back from challenging the assumptions of the boulevard about class distinctions. 'I'm so very, very sorry', Jane says at the news of Fanny's wonderful offers, a startling remark in which Coward flunks taking sides on the issue of social mobility. 'Something seems to have gone out of all of us, and I'm not sure I like what's left.' Ideas are quickly defused by sentiment. The 'issue' of class becomes dramatically 'irrelevant' (JANE. 'You needn't worry about Fanny and Joe any more Ellen') when a telegram arrives announcing Joe Marryot's death on the battlefield. Fade out on social issues, fade in on private grief made historically spectacular as Jane 'like a sleepwalker', moves amidst the Armistice celebrations in Trafalgar Square with rattle and squeaker. The yoking together of jubilation and grief, the sheer onslaught of massed emotion is overwhelming. The stage direction calls for the yelling to slowly fade away.

'JANE is left, still cheering and occasionally brandishing the rattle and blowing the squeaker. But she can't be heard at all because the full strength of the orchestra is playing 'Land of Hope and Glory'.

The second act curtain falls on this moment of stage-managed bittersweet sentiment. It was the scene's impact, not its insights which pleased Coward. 'The Trafalgar Square scene', he wrote; 'obvious, not quite psychologically accurate, but undeniably effective, all that noise and movement against "Land of Hope and Glory".'[27]

Coward felt *Cavalcade* 'possessed two or three really well-written scenes, notably the funeral of Queen Victoria and the outbreak of the war in 1914'.[28] As the Marryots prepare to watch the Queen's funeral cortege from their balcony, the dialogue works against the immensity of the occasion.

JOE [*the smaller, younger son*]: Why did Queen Victoria die, Mum?
JANE: Because she was a very old lady, and very tired.
JOE: Could I have another piece of cake?

What makes the scene riveting is not the words but Coward's eye for stage pattern: the hand that composes and recomposes the tableau. The flutter of expectation changes as the funeral approaches. The boys, their parents, the Bridges stand suddenly rigid on the balcony. The music of the cortege swells as the band and the clatter of horses pass directly beneath them. The noise gives way to silence. In that aural effect, the significance of the event is theatrically clinched.

JANE: Five kings riding behind her.
JOE: Mum, she must have been a very little lady.
    The lights fade.

The enchantment of *Cavalcade* is in Coward's fancy fili-gree work – his use of space, sound, silence and groupings to evoke a world. No Coward play is as scenic as *Cavalcade*. Some of Coward's narrative images would become cine-matic clichés. The Marryots' eldest son Edward and his new bride, Edith, lean on the railing of an ocean liner discussing their happiness. At the end of the scene, Edith picks up her cloak which has been covering a life-belt, 'the words S.S. Titanic can be seen in black letters on the white. The lights fade into complete darkness, but the letters remain glowing.' In *Post-Mortem*, words failed Coward to convey his disgust at chauvinism and at the waste of life. In *Cavalcade*, he abandoned words and conveyed the irony brilliantly with sound and image (II,7):

Above the proscenium 1914 glows in lights. It changes to 1915, 1916, 1917, and 1918. Meanwhile, soldiers march uphill endlessly. Out of darkness into darkness. Sometimes they sing gay songs, sometimes they whistle, sometimes they march silently, but the sound of their tramping feet is unceasing. Below, the vision of them brightly-dressed, energetic women appear in pools of light singing stirring recruiting songs – 'Sunday I walk out with a soldier', 'We don't want to lose you', etc. With 1918 they fade away, as also does the vision of the soldiers, although the soldiers can still be heard very far off, marching and singing their songs.

Although Coward's dialogue in *Cavalcade* has been rightly slated for its 'crushing obviousness',[29] *Cavalcade* is intended more as a feast for the eye and ear. His massive stage pictures give simple plot points a poignant resonance and make an asset out of his theatrical limitation. At the finale, the remaining Marryots and Bridges are at a night-club listening to Fanny sing. Coward perches her above them on the piano, a grouping which intimates yet another shift in the family histories. Fanny is the new rising spirit of democracy and disillusion. The room is 'angular and strange'; the song is 'discordant'; when people dance afterwards, it is 'the dull dancing of habit'. Every sight, every motion, every sound, every position is orchestrated by Coward to create the sense of a disjointed world. The night club allows him smoothly to knit together the past and the present, while a Riley light above the stage spells out the headlines Fanny sings about:

We've reached a deadline
The Press headline – every sorrow,
Blues value is News value to-morrow.

As the song fades, *Cavalcade* begins its final, long cinematic dissolve:

... The lights fade away from everything but the dancers, who appear to be rising in the air. They disappear, and down stage

102

left six 'incurables' in blue hospital uniform are sitting making baskets. They disappear, and FANNY is seen singing her song for a moment, then far way up stage a jazz band is seen playing wildly. Then down stage JANE and ROBERT standing with glasses of champagne held aloft; then ELLEN sitting in front of a Radio loud speaker ... The visions are repeated quicker and quicker, while across the darkness a Riley light sign spelling out the news ...

The progression of repeated images moves the play out of history into nightmare; then from 'darkness and silence' into Coward's own form of patriotic prophecy. 'I do hope, profoundly hope, that this country will find dignity, greatness and peace again – no cheapness there, that came from the heart', Coward wrote. 'Or perhaps, from the roots – twisted sentimental roots, stretching a long way down and a long way back, too deep to be unearthed by intelligence or pacific reason or even contempt, there, embedded for life.'[30]

Entertainment is not politically neutral, but Coward thought so. 'The prime purpose of the theatre is entertainment', he said. 'If, by any chance, a playwright wishes to express a political opinion or a moral opinion or a philosophy, he must be a good enough craftsman to do it with so much spice of entertainment in it that the public get the message without being aware of it. The moment the public sniffs propaganda, they stay away and I am all in favour of the public coming to the theatre, paying for their seats at the box office, and enjoying themselves.'[31]

Nobody sees their own point of view as propaganda, certainly not Coward. But neither frivolity nor patriotism are neutral. The popularity of his plays reinforce the *status quo*, that most entrenched of political positions.

After *Cavalcade*, which lavishly honoured public suffering (JANE. 'Let's drink to our sons who made part of the pattern and to our hearts who died with them ...'), Coward wrote *Design for Living* which was frivolous about suffering.

Both plays shy away from suffering, either public or private. Frivolity is the laughter of a detached mind. At the end of the decade, Coward again wrote two apparently disparate plays but with the same concomitant evasiveness, intended to be performed on alternate nights. In *Present Laughter*, Coward starred as the posturing egotistical matinee idol Garry Essendine. In *This Happy Breed*, Coward cast himself as a decent, hard-working, ordinary British bloke, Frank Gibbons. In Essendine's world, fame and money insulate him from the vagaries of life. Essendine's comic mission is escape, to escape the fans, the would-be lovers and playwrights, and all the other small-fry of ordinary life that intrude on the routine of his success. In *This Happy Breed*, Frank Gibbons may not have the trappings of worldly success, but he spouts the rich man's faith in the just order of things. '. . . The country got tired, it's tired now', Frank tells his son Reg, who's been taking part in the General Strike while his father has been out strike-breaking by manning a bus. 'And it's up to us ordinary people to keep things steady.'

'*This Happy Breed* is a suburban middle-class comedy covering the period between the Armstice in 1918', Coward wrote, 'to the humiliating year of 1938, when the late Neville Chamberlain spent so much time in the air. Many of the critics detected in this play an attitude on my part of amused patronage and condescension toward the habits and manners of suburban London. They implied that in setting the play in a milieu so far removed from the cocktail and caviar stratum where I so obviously belonged, I was over-reaching myself and writing about people far removed from my superficial comprehension. In this, as usual, they were quite wrong'.[32] The critics were perhaps not completely on the wrong track. It was not the people, but the social reality of their world from which Coward was now so far removed. This forced Coward to sentimentalize Frank Gibbons and turn him into a political Pollyanna. The play is an appeal to middle-class decency: an appeal, as one critic rightly has

104

observed, 'from above to above, pretending by mimetic means, to come from below'.[33]

In three acts, with each act divided into three scenes, *This Happy Breed* is constructed according to Coward's familiar symmetry. Each scene jumps Frank Gibbons and the dramas of his household ahead in time. With each leap forward comes a shift in their relationship. As in *Cavalcade*, Coward's slick technique is to personalize history so that emotion replaces analysis. His characters are always on the outskirts of events. History is a backdrop rather than an issue.

The play begins in 1919 with Gibbons, only recently de-mobbed, moving into his new house in Clapham Common. With the memory of carnage behind him, he has lost his faith in God, but not the belief that 'there isn't going to be another war'. His next-door neighbour, Bob Mitchell, turns out to be an acquaintance from the trenches. They end the first scene with an old *Cavalcade* ironic fillip, toasting 'Happy Days'. Gibbons has 'seen too much' in the war; and his staunch contentment with English life has its basis in forgetfulness. But even in the calm of Clapham, history catches up with him. Other scenes are Gibbons coming home from the General Strike breaking (1926); Gibbons listening to the King's abdication speech (1936); Gibbons hearing Neville Chamberlain praised; and his daughter, Vi, going off to celebrate Chamberlain's Munich agreement in Trafalgar Square. In this survey of the recent past, there is no talk of Nazism or Fascism; and a great deal of special pleading for 'being English' and speaking 'horse sense'.

Having only recently 'arrived', Coward didn't want to go back; and Gibbons is another cleverly disguised mouthpiece for a static society. Gibbons is as secure in his station at the lower-middle end of British society as Essendine at the top of it. Each has a fierce sense of his place in the scheme of things. Gibbons passes on his almost feudal vision of social inertia to all his children. Coward means it to show his tolerant, good sense. Reg, going through a socialist phase in

105

the twenties, gets his father's don't-rock-the-boat-speech. Queenie, the well-named eldest daughter, gets her father's mind-your-place peroration. A manicurist, Queenie refuses to marry Bob Mitchell's son, Billy, in the twenties because she wants a different kind of life, and he doesn't then seem to have prospects. She has 'airs and graces' and admits her restlessness to Billy when she turns him down: 'I hate washing up and helping Mum darn Dad's socks and listening to Aunt Sylvia keeping on about how ill she is all the time, and what's more I know why I hate it too, it's because it's all so common!'

Queenie runs off with a married Major only later to be ditched in Brussels and remarried in the last scenes to Billy, whose perseverance towards her is another example of true Brit decency. But before she sets off for greener pastures, Gibbons gives her a piece of his mind. 'You're trying to be something you're not', Frank tells Queenie, when she admits that living in a suburb 'is not good enough for me'. He continues: '... One of these days when you know a bit more, you'll find out that there are worse things than being ordinary and respectable and living the way you've been brought up to live'. Coward, of course, lived a star's life and had a star's faith in his own singularity. And Gibbons' attitude well-served the star mentality which depends on the idea of the extraordinariness of the few standing out from the ordinariness of the many.

Coward's narrative structure allows the passage of time to work its own ironies. It is not only people who change over the years. Objects and incidents take on their own resonance. 'Bit of luck about the May tree, isn't it?' Frank says (I,1) to his wife Ethel when they first arrive. But the leaves of the May tree brought indoors (II.3) in 1932 are the ill-omen that foreshadows Reg's death in a car crash. In the same way, Frank Gibbons' attitude toward war echoes through the scenes and returns to haunt him.

He begins with a firm conviction that the Great War is the last war. By 1932 (II,2), Gibbons is wondering to Bob

Mitchell: 'I wonder when the next war will be'. And Mitchell replies: 'Not in our lifetime, nor in our son's, thank God!' In 1919, it was Gibbons who was saying 'Everything more than all right, it's wonderful'. But by 1931 the audience hears a hint of doubt in Frank's words when Bob Mitchell expresses the same satisfaction.

> BOB: Well, we've got a brand new Government now and every-thing in the garden's lovely.
> FRANK (*raising the glass*): Here's hoping!

By 1938, Gibbons is branded a 'war monger' by his sister Sylvia because he's suspicious of Chamberlain's 'peace with honour'. Coward uses the incident to let Gibbons mouth his own political opinions which, off the stage, some of Coward's acquaintances like Chips Channon found 'quite out of date':[34]

> I've seen thousands of people, English people, mark you! carry-ing on like maniacs, shouting and cheering with relief, for no other reason but that they'd been thoroughly frightened, and it made me sick and that's a fact! I only hope to God that we shall have guts enough to learn one lesson from this and that we shall never find ourselves in a position again when we have to appease anybody!

At the finale (1939), Gibbons is once again moving house. With the outbreak of war, his world too is undergoing a radical revision. In Act One (I,1), Ethel had asked him about war, 'Would you go again?' And Gibbons answered, 'I expect so'. Now twenty years on and too old to fight, he imparts the same patriotic fighting spirit to his baby grandson and namesake who lies in a pram in the nearly empty Clapham house. 'People ... go on about peace and good will and ideals they believe in', Frank tells the boy, about how the English have got 'soft and afraid'. 'But so-mehow don't seem to believe in 'em enough to think they're worth fighting for ... The trouble with the world is, Frankie, that there are too many ideals and too little horse sense...'

In this soliloquy, Coward is showing Gibbons Sr. and Jnr. redeemed by each other. Coward's technique never falters. The image of the older generation talking to the new one about what it means to be British is so emotional that it sweeps the audience unquestioningly along with Coward's dogmatic commonplaces about the national predicament. 'You belong to a race that's been bossy for years, and the reason it's held on as long as it has is that nine times out of ten it's behaved decently and treated people right', Gibbons says, recapitulating the imperial myth and dismissing centuries of slavery and exploitation in one sly and weighted sentence.

The stage picture of continuity underlines Gibbons' rallying cry and call to arms. Coward was never as eloquent about change as stasis. In a time of national crisis, his curtain speech was unabashedly conservative. His monologue ends not talking about fighting to make a better world but keeping what he (and Coward) already felt was a damn good one:

> ... the people themselves, the ordinary people like you and me, know something better than all the fussy old politicians put together – we know what we belong to, where we come from, and where we're going. We may not know it with our brains, but we know it with our roots. And we know another thing too, and it's this. We 'aven't lived and died and struggled all these hundreds of years to get decency and justice and freedom for ourselves without being prepared to fight fifty wars if need be – to keep 'em.

When war broke out in September, 1939, Coward scrapped his production plans for *Present Laughter* and *This Happy Breed* (they were finally mounted in rep with *Blithe Spirit* in 1942) and threw himself into the war effort. As Coward recounts in *Future Indefinite*, he found it hard at first to find a niche for himself. In 1939, he'd been dispatched to Paris to help set up a propaganda unit in cooperation with the Commissariat d'Information. The German Occupation of Paris put an end to that job. And Coward spent frustrating months in America without any authorized mission. He had hoped for something in Intelligence: but it was claimed he was too famous for such secret work. Coward found no favour in high places. And, after passing on information garnered at dinner with President and Mrs. Roosevelt, Coward's action caused questions to be raised in Parliament and the *Sunday Express* railed, '... Mr. Noël Coward as special emissary to the States can do nothing but harm. In any event, Mr Coward is not the man for the job. His flippant England – cocktails, countesses, caviar – has gone'.[35] Coward returned to Britain resigned to being a cheerleader on the sidelines of the field of battle. No sooner was he back in England than Coward was on the BBC in 1940, invoking his curtain speech from *Cavalcade* and painting a gallant picture of the British at war. 'It seems that for the first time people of all shapes and sizes, classes and creeds are getting to know one another. Never before was there such richness, such an awareness of adventure. Here we are on our little island and the issues have become simple ...' Coward said, concluding: 'I maintain that it is not only a pretty exciting thing to be English, but critical as well because on this side of the world it is all there is left'.[36]

The war did indeed make things simple and cast a cold light on the political nature of stardom and entertainment. The public loved Coward because he inspired hope and pleasure. He may have been unwanted as an ambassador but he was needed as a spellbinder. The leaders used his performing talents to consolidate public opinion and raise morale. Churchill told Coward to sing his songs to the troops while the guns were firing; and in the end, Coward did just that, and more. 'I behaved through most of the war with gallantry tinged, I suspect, by a strong urge to show off',[37] he said. He had invented himself, his own stage idiom, his brand of high comedy; and, aided by a pianist and a crowded global itinerary, Coward invented his war.

'When I set out on my incessant journeys round the globe', he wrote, 'a spate of lyrics gushed out of me'.[38] They had to; Coward needed new material. His solo act ran an hour and a half, and he 'frequently performed four or five times a day'.[39] War focused Coward's instinct for sentiment and satire. Soon the English were hearing Coward's 'London Pride' memorably cheering them:

Stay, city
Smokily enchanted
Cradle of our memories and hopes and fears.
Every Blitz
Your resistance
Toughening
From the Ritz
To the Anchor and Crown,
Nothing ever could override
The pride of London Town.

But courage wants to laugh. During the war, Coward added a number of brilliant satiric songs whose wit has found their way from the stage to the pages of dictionaries of quotations. Coward mythologized England as he teased it. 'I loved its follies and apathies and curious streaks of genius; I loved standing to attention for "God Save the King"; I loved British courage, British humour, and British understatement; I loved the justice, efficiency and even the dullness of British Colonial Administration ...'[40] Even at its most mischievous, Coward's laughter never broke faith with the society:

Have you had any word
Of that bloke in the 'Third',
Was it Southerby, Sedgwick or Sim?
They had him thrown out of the club in Bombay
For, apart from his mess-bills exceeding his pay,
He took to pig-sticking in *quite* the wrong way.
I wonder what happened to him!

110

Coward's political plays never had the élan, the detachment, the playfulness or the impact of the songs which corrupted the public with pleasure. (The Nazis had Coward on their liquidation list.)[41] The War made Coward aware of laughter and song as political weapons. 'Defeat is a state of mind', says a member of the English Resistance in *Peace In Our Time* (1947), Coward's political melodrama which strains to imagine England occupied by the Germans. In the play, an SS leader asks an English woman what 'caustic irony' means, and she answers: 'A secret weapon ... Laced with humour and hatred, it can sometimes be very effective'. The play manages only an off-stage incident of this potent mix. The English Resistance sneak 'Whose Afraid of the Big Bad Wolf' on a newsreel of Hitler and leave the Nazis covered in confusion. Coward's 'Don't Let's Be Beastly to the Germans' perfects the coruscating ridicule *Peace in Our Time* only describes. Although the song's brilliant irony was misunderstood when it was first broadcast in 1943, Coward's wit when mixed with hatred for the appeasers and the Germans could be as withering as he claimed:

Don't let's be beastly to the Germans
When our victory is ultimately won,
It was just those nasty Nazis who persuaded them to fight
And their Beethoven and Bach are really far worse than their
     bite
Let's be meek to them –
And turn the other cheek to them
And try to bring out their latent sense of fun.
Let's give them full air parity –
And treat the rats with charity,
But don't let's be beastly to the Hun.

When Coward returned to England to join the war effort, he invoked the Common Man as an explanation to his distraught mother who wanted him to stay in America. He was working, Coward told her, 'for the country itself and for the ordinary people who belong to it ... I wanted to be here to experience what all the people I know and all the millions of people I don't know are experiencing'.[42] He also wanted to make 'a *lasting* contribution' to the War [my italics].

Quickly written and vastly popular, Coward's songs did not fulfil his ambitions for himself in the war. In later years, it would irritate him that the songs held such prominence in the Coward canon. In war, as in peacetime, Coward wanted his contribution to be as a writer.

Coward got his chance in 1942 when he wrote, produced, starred in and co-directed the film *In Which We Serve*, a story about a torpedoed destroyer and the lives of those who serve her. It was also an act of homage to Lord Mountbatten (and the crew of the HMS Kelly) after the mischief of *Hands Across the Sea*. Coward referred to the film as 'a naval *Cavalcade*',[43] and its success was as unequivocal. Considered one of the finest pieces of English Navy war propaganda, the film was also hailed in the press as 'the best war film yet made in England or America',[44] an assessment which forty years on seems insupportable.

Coward played the ship's captain who, along with other exhausted and wounded crewmen of the *Torrin*, cling to a raft while their lives flash before them. The cinematic cross-cutting between public and private history in *Cavalcade* is worked in the film to greater effect. With the ship as a backdrop, the audience hears Chamberlain announcing the outbreak of war, sees it rescuing men from Dunkirk, watches sea battles. Meanwhile, the tapestry of the men's lives evokes and reinforces Coward's boulevard belief in the seamless pattern of the English class system. It was a notion of stratified unity that only the war could make credible. 'The *Torrin* is gone', Coward wrote in the publicity note for the film. 'And so have many of her crew. But they, no less than the survivors, carry on the fight. For they are the spirit of the British Navy, past, present and future, which will guard our shores and keep our honour on all the oceans of the world ... There will always be other ships and men to sail them. It is these men, in peace or war, to whom we owe so much . . .'[45]

The War aroused great patriotic emotions to which Coward was susceptible and which he made memorably eloquent. In peacetime these impulses were submerged by his frivolity and ironic understatement. In crisis, they demanded to be said straightforwardly. As Captain of the *Torrin*, Coward got to speak out for England in his final farewell scene to his men. The speech knits together Coward's sense of duty and hard work with his belief in the gallantry and resilience of the Englishman.

> . . . There may be less than half the *Torrin* left, but I feel that we'll all take up the battle with even stronger heart. Each of us knows twice as much about fighting, and each of us has twice as good a reason to fight. You will all be sent to replace men who've been killed in other ships and the next time you're in action remember the *Torrin*. There isn't one of you that I wouldn't be proud and honoured to serve with again. Goodbye, good luck and thank you all from the bottom of my heart.

An actor is a technician of the spirit. Coward's war effort was to help consolidate and raise the morale of the nation. His battles were fought in front of thousands of weary, entertainment-starved troops and in the Denham Studios where *In Which We Serve* was made. He won no medals for bravery; but instead, in 1943, he was awarded a special Academy Award for 'outstanding production achievement' in a film that memorialized the bravery of others.

4

Ghosts in the Fun Machine

'When we act out the hostile aggression of our dead, we draw of course on our aggression toward them ... We make them go away because they have lost *us*. But by making them go away, by transforming them from malign to benign spirits, we also transform or banish our aggression toward them.'
– Michael Goldman, *The Actor's Freedom*

Ghosts abound in Coward's plays. They appear to warn, to prophesy, and 'to personify men's hopes and fears, making explicit a great deal which could not be said directly'.[1] In *Cavalcade* and *Post-Mortem* the stage ghosts serve the ghost's traditional social function of ensuring reverence for the dead. At the finale of *Cavalcade*, just before the play toasts England's future glory, ghosts of the past loom up in spectral, disembodied stage pictures. The stage effect takes the characters out of time. They become emblematic apparitions who confront and mourn both past and present. And in *Shadow Play* (1936), apparitions of the quarrelling Gayforths appear in a dream to recall their romantic past and rekindle their threatened love. These 'shadows' function as guarantors of 'general moral standards, sustaining good relations and disturbing the sleep of the guilty'.[2]

Coward was fascinated by death. 'I've witnessed death many times', he said, discussing his hobby of observing surgery. 'I once had a man die in my arms'.[3] In *Private Lives*, Elyot says to Amanda, 'Death is very laughable really, such a cunning little mystery. All done with mirrors'. Death, as Coward joked, was something to be overcome. The war only intensified this feeling. 'The English do not always take their

114

pleasure sadly', Coward wrote in his diary, of the dancing on Plymouth Hoe after a bad blitz. 'At least not when they are surrounded by death and destruction.'[4] Coward's obsession with output was not just a means of 'killing time' but of cheating death. A writer's work is his ghost; and Coward took solace in the belief that his spirit would haunt the world long after his body had departed it. He put this hankering into verse:

> I'm here for a short visit only
> And I'd rather be loved than hated
> Eternity may be lonely
> When my body's disintegrated
> And that which is loosely termed my soul
> Goes whizzing off through the infinite
> By means of some vague, remote control
> I'd like to think I was missed a bit.[5]

He was more adamant and less modest to Cecil Beaton in 1942 when their chat turned to playwrighting. Beaton's diary reports:

> [Coward] admitted to having had such success during the last fifteen years that he wouldn't think it terrible if a bomb killed him today. '*Blithe Spirit* is a bloody good play, and *Private Lives* will always be revived and go into the history of comedy like a play by Congreve or Wilde.'[6]

It was not hard for Coward to imagine his own death when a blitzed London was filled with the sights and smells of destruction. The shock was all the greater to Coward who returned to London in 1941, having been away from war-torn England since September 1939 on various official and unofficial war assignments. 'Abbey hit, also Houses of Parliament. Smell of burning everywhere',[7] Coward wrote in his diary. And later: 'The whole city a pitiful sight'.[8] For the first time the imminence of death was a fact of life. Fear and rage came out in Coward as mockery; and on 16 April he met with producer Binkie Beaumont. 'Told him I had an

idea for a comedy and would try to get away and write it.'[9]
The comedy had both its symbolic and practical purposes;
a means of keeping the Grim Reaper and the creditors at
bay. 'Spent morning with Lorn discussing financial troubles
which are considerable', Coward wrote in his diary on 22
April. 'Also discussed play as possible solution. Title *Blithe
Spirit*. Very gay, superficial comedy about a ghost. Feel it
may be good.'

From his diary accounts, Coward had the play in mind
for some time. But Coward later wrote that the comedy
materialized with eery serendipity:

> I shall ever be grateful for the almost psychic gift that enabled
> me to write *Blithe Spirit* in five days during one of the darkest
> years of the war. [Coward writes in *Play Parade 5*.] It was not
> meticulously constructed in advance and only one day elapsed
> between its original conception and the moment I sat down to
> write it. It fell into my mind and on to the manuscript. Six weeks
> later it was produced and ran for four and a half years.[10]

Coward began *Blithe Spirit* on 3 May and finished it on
9 May 1941. 'Really feel I have done a rousing good
comedy',[11] Coward wrote in his diary, of the play in which
two wifely ghosts are materialized to torment their former
husband. Coward's adjective for success is significant. Tradi-
tionally ghosts return to rouse. Ghosts are trapped, restless
energy. Emblems of memory, ghosts are also catalysts of
consciousness. As a stage device, ghosts inspire aggression
and action. In tragedy, the panic they generate becomes
revenge for injustice; in comedy, they add disorder to order
so as to give a sense of the whole. Ghosts dramatize the fact
that the dead are very much part of life. In making a spectacle of coming to terms with ghosts, the stage acts out an
ancient shamanistic function of winning power over the
dead. The ghosts who are materialized in *Blithe Spirit* are
ghosts of ruthless passion and tyrannical order, forces that
vied as much for control of Coward's life as Charles Condomine's. The situation released a passion, inventiveness

and energy in Coward which his playwrighting would never again equal. In the battle between the ghostly suffocation of the wives and Condomine's manipulative charm, the play becomes a paradigm of survivor guilt. In the end, Condomine engineers a victory over the ghosts, and puts fear, guilt and mourning behind him.

Charles Condomine is haunted for his selfishness, and long before the ghosts of his former wives face him with his exploitation, the audience sees him getting ready to exploit Madame Arcati, whom he had cajoled into having a seance at his house so he can observe her for his novel. In his own way, Condomine is as unscrupulous as the forces who later beset him. The curtain goes up on the Condomine living room where Ruth, and later Charles, are setting the stage for their manipulation of Madame Arcati. The first sentences of the play are Ruth's instructions to the maid to slow down and act normally. Edith sprints everywhere, a signal – the audience later realizes – of her mediumship. Ruth, a stickler for order, tells her: 'When you're serving, Edith, try to remember to do it calmly and methodically'. Charles too has some stage directions for the charade they're about to enact. The guests – the Bradmans – have already been warned and Charles gives Ruth the same notes on her performance. 'You must be dead serious, and if possible a little intense,' he tells her. The Bradmans, as Ruth says, 'are as sceptical as we are'. Mixing himself a dry martini, Condomine toasts his next novel 'To *The Unseen*'. The irony (which Coward underlines by having Ruth say, 'That's a wonderful title') is two-fold. Not only is he about to be visited by the ghost of his former wife; but by the end of his struggle with ghosts, his own unseen nature will be revealed. He is detached from the dead, and he feels guilty about it. When Ruth asks if it hurts when he thinks about his first wife, Elvira, Condomine answers: 'No, not really – sometimes I almost wish it did – I feel rather guilty'. A modern man, Condomine displays the estrangement of the community of the living from the community of the dead. This change of

117

cultural attitudes had a direct bearing on ghosts. 'The main reason for the disappearance of ghosts', Keith Thomas writes of the decline in belief in them, 'is that the society is no longer responsive to the presumed wishes of past generations'.[12]

Coward does not hurry his hijinx. In the exchanges prior to the arrival of Madame Arcati in Act One, he establishes both the character of Condomine's second wife, and the nature of both his marriages. His first wife, Elvira, died after just five years of marriage. Now seven years on, Condomine seems to be ambivalent. 'I remember her physical attractiveness, which was tremendous, and her spiritual integrity which was nil', he tells Ruth, who, as the second wife, tries hard to be mature and hide her inclination to jealousy. Condomine continues: 'I remember how morally untidy she was'.

There is nothing untidy about Ruth. Her first entrance demonstrates her efficiency ('RUTH comes in centre briskly', the stage directions read '... She is dressed for dinner but not elaborately'.) She too has been previously married. She is realistic about her new partnership and aware that there was a more physical passion between Elvira and Charles. Although Charles vows his love to Ruth with great charm, she insists 'not the wildest stretch of the imagination could describe it as the first fine careless rapture'. She goes on: 'We're neither of us adolescent, Charles ... careless rapture at this stage would be incongruous and embarrassing'. As they fence about their feelings, the dialogue hints at an emptiness. They are entrenched in their maturity. Mystery and passion elude them.

> RUTH: You're very annoying, you know you are – when I said 'Poor Elvira' it came from the heart – you must have bewildered her so horribly.
> CHARLES: Don't I ever bewilder you at all.
> RUTH: Never for an instant – I know every trick.

Elvira slips too often into their conversation. Charles parries

Ruth's questions with charm; and Ruth fishes for reassurance by comparing herself to Elvira. Coward shrewdly makes this situation do double duty. Their conversation not only reveals their character but sets out the irony on which the plot turns:

> RUTH: If I died, I wonder how long it would be before you married again?
> CHARLES: You won't die – you're not the dying sort.
> RUTH: Neither was Elvira.
> CHARLES: Oh yes, she was, now that I look back on it – she had a certain ethereal, not quite of this world quality – nobody could call you even remotely ethereal.
> RUTH: Nonsense – she was of the earth, earthy.
> CHARLES: Well she is now, anyhow.
> RUTH: You know that's the kind of observation that shocks people.
> CHARLES: It's discouraging to think how many people are shocked by honesty and how few by deceit.

The word 'deceit' is passed off by both parties as a general statement. 'Write that down', Ruth tells Charles. 'You might forget it'. But, as events reveal, they are living it.

There is nothing deceitful about Madame Arcati. She has nothing to hide, and hides nothing. Her eccentricities are apparent for all to see. A 'striking woman dressed not too extravagantly but with a decided bias towards the barbaric', Madame Arcati's passion for bike riding, dry martinis, and the spirit world stamps her immediately as an innocent. She is in direct contrast to the rest of the sceptical company. 'I really do think you should try to have a little faith', Charles says to Ruth sardonically earlier on. 'Life without faith is an arid business.' Madame Arcati is a true believer. Irony is not her mode. 'Don't worry, dear', she tells Mrs. Bradman. 'I am quite used to sceptics.' She is all business. When Dr. Bradman hears that Madame Arcati's spiritual contact is a child called Daphne who died in 1884, he makes a little joke: 'She must be long in the tooth, I should think'. Madame

Arcati flies at him. 'You should think, Dr. Bradman, but I fear you don't – at least, not profoundly enough.' Her blunt sincerity, the high seriousness with which she undertakes her eccentric calling is the source of her comedy. She is not intimidated by people or ghosts. 'Daphne is really more attached to Irving Berlin than anybody else', she says rummaging through Charles's records for music to conjure the right mood. 'She likes a tune she can hum – ah, here's one – "Always".' Charles's agitation at the choice of song (he 'half jumps up again') is the first clue that he is haunted by Elvira even before she is materialized.

Coward has great fun with Madame Arcati's hocus-pocus. She rushes about the room to turn out the lights. She is tormented by Daphne. She becomes progressively more hysterical as the table emits a series of thumps from the other world. Madame Arcati is pushed off her stool by the poltergeist and then the table is overturned. Elvira's first words, spoken in the dark with 'a very charming voice' are a tyrannical command: 'Leave it where it is'.

In theatrical terms, Elvira is a brilliant manifestation of comic aggression. Through her, Coward can tease normality and flaunt his maliciousness. Elvira has returned to possess Charles and persecute Ruth, thereby incorporating into contemporary comedy the ancient aims of propitiating *and* expelling ghosts. Elvira's antics escalate from mischief to murder. At her first entrance, Coward's stage picture links her freedom to the licence of the dead.

> She is charmingly dressed in a sort of negligée. Everything about her is grey: hair, skin, dress, hands, so we must accept the fact that she is not quite of this world. She passes between DR. and MRS. BRADMAN and RUTH while they are talking. None of them see her. She goes up stage and sits soundlessly on a chair. She regards them with interest, a slight smile on her face.

With Elvira and Ruth both demanding attention, Charles (who is the only one who can see and hear Elvira) quickly becomes the servant of two masters. In trying to censor the comments of the unseen, Charles also becomes self-conscious. The situation is a recipe for fiasco; and also a paradigm of homosexual consciousness. Although Coward keeps the comedy light, the predicament takes its passion and resonance from its thinly veiled connection to the schizophrenic quality of homosexual life. The double-bind is personified by the ghost. Ruthless, volatile, irresistible, Elvira is passion incarnate. Having contained and hidden and re-translated his own passion, Coward also makes her a projection of murdered instinct returned to haunt the writer. Elvira's havoc is characterized as blithe but underneath the gaiety is something lethal. Charles is alternatively tormented by passion and invalidated by those who won't accept it.

CHARLES (*moves a couple of paces towards RUTH*): Elvira is here, Ruth – she's standing a few yards away from you.
RUTH (*sarcastically*): Yes, dear, I can see her distinctly – under the piano with a zebra!
CHARLES: But, Ruth ...
RUTH: I am not going to stay here arguing any longer ...
ELVIRA: Hurray!
CHARLES: Shut up!
RUTH (*incensed*): How dare you speak to me like that!
CHARLES: Listen, Ruth – please listen –
RUTH: I will not listen to any more of this nonsense. ...

At first Charles tries to make Elvira behave. As Elvira remarks, he is 'unwelcoming and disagreeable'. He tries to silence her. He curses her. He denies her. 'This is obviously a hallucination, isn't it?' he says. His attempts at control only magnify Elvira's power and his impotence to contain it. Finally, with Ruth storming out of the room in a huff, he admits Elvira's ghostly presence. The audience learns that Elvira is and always has been Charles's hidden passion:

CHARLES: What happens if I touch you?
ELVIRA: I doubt if you can. Do you want to?
CHARLES (*sits left end of the sofa*): Oh Elvira ... (*He buries his face in his hands.*)

121

The moment is filled with longing and surprise. Charles's charm has kept his own feelings hidden. His deception is suddenly apparent. As with all other Coward comedy couples, Elvira and Charles cannot live happily together or apart. They recap their contentious marital history:

ELVIRA: ... you hit me with a billiard cue.
CHARLES: Only very, very gently.

It is a replay of Elyot and Amanda in *Private Lives*, but with a difference. Being a ghost, Elvira has an added symbolic dimension, at once a person and a subconscious wish. Untouchable and omnipotent, she is the erotic ideal which can never be captured. Charles falls quite literally under this erotic spell. 'I suppose I shall wake up eventually', he says, lying back on the sofa. And a few lines later he drowsily suggests, '... If I'm really out of my mind they'll put me in an asylum'. Although the scene plays itself out quietly, the excellent curtain lines to Act One announce the possessiveness of this spirit of repressed passion which is the basis for the violent struggle to come:

CHARLES (*very drowsily indeed*): Poor Ruth...
RUTH (*gently and sweetly*): To hell with Ruth.
CURTAIN.

Act Two begins with Charles buoyantly celebrating a return to normality. He stands by the window in the morning light. 'It's extraordinary about daylight, isn't it,' he says. 'The way it reduces everything to normal.' Even though Elvira is not present, she dominates conversation between Charles and Ruth. Elvira's playful, relaxed, charming presence in Act One is in direct contrast to Ruth's in Act Two. Overnight she has become 'glacial', grave, and haughty ('I wish you wouldn't be facetious with the servants Charles – it confuses and undermines their morale'). Charles tries to explain the 'aberration'. But Ruth chalks it up to drink. At this point, Charles begins to haunt Ruth as he himself is haunted. He takes liberties. He becomes tyrannical and insulting. 'Women! My God, what I think of women!' he explodes, complaining of Ruth's jealousy about Elvira's attractiveness. Ruth accuses him of being hag-ridden. And Charles explodes, 'The only woman in my whole life who's ever attempted to dominate me is you – you've been at it for years.' He continues: 'You boss me and bully me and order me about – you won't even allow me to have an hallucination if I want to'. But Ruth completely discounts Charles and his criticism. 'Charles, alcohol will ruin your whole life if you allow it to get hold of you, you know.' Charles is at stalemate.

Elvira's presence has made Charles 'profoundly uneasy'. Even before she reappears in Act Two, Charles fears his abnormality. 'There is something wrong with me,' he tells Ruth. 'Something fundamentally wrong with me.' But his identity is not yet severely threatened. Ruth seems concerned and suggests Charles see a psychoanalyst. 'I refuse to endure months of expensive humiliation only to be told at the end of it that at the age of four I was in love with my rocking horse.' There's nothing to be done. Ruth questions him about how he feels now, and Charles answers: 'Apart from being worried I feel quite normal.' At this point, Elvira enters to persecute these notions of normality. The inability of the characters to agree on what reality is drives them crazy.

Elvira enters with a bunch of grey roses 'that are as grey as the rest of her' and immediately starts to take ghostly liberties by throwing out Ruth's zinnias in favour of her deathly roses. Charles starts to speak to Elvira, and to Ruth he seems like a jabbering madman. The presence of a ghost reworks the convention of mistaken identities. Charles's confusion at seeing Elvira makes him seem 'dead' to Ruth. Her husband is transformed before her eyes. While Coward doesn't exploit the machinery of farce to show identity disintegrating as the momentum of coincidence increases, his characters jump to the same conclusions as they do in farce. 'Every form of drama has its rendezvous with madness,'

Eric Bentley writes in his famous essay on farce. 'If drama shows extreme situations, *the* extreme situation for human beings – short of death – is the point where sanity gives out.'[13] Charles is pushed to the breaking point as he exhorts Elvira to mind her own business, a statement which is instantly misinterpreted by Ruth who thinks it's addressed to her:

CHARLES: Please mind your own business.
RUTH: If you behaving like a lunatic isn't my business nothing is.
ELVIRA: I expect it was about me, wasn't it? I know I ought to feel sorry but I'm not – I'm delighted.
CHARLES: How can you be so inconsiderate.
RUTH (*shrilly*): Inconsiderate! I like that I must say –

Ruth clings tenaciously to her view of things; and Charles' attempts to reason with her end in a hilarious stand-off. Ruth thinks Charles has gone mad. 'Of course, darling,' she says, trying to jolly him up to bed. 'We'll all be quiet, won't we? We'll be as quiet as little mice.' He is completely double-binded. In order to break the impasse, Charles begs Elvira to prove her presence. 'Promise you'll do what I ask?' he says. Elvira, who's given to waltzing around the room while everything around her is in chaos, torments Ruth. She shoves a vase of flowers under her nose, then slams the windows in her face. Ruth is 'hysterical', then 'really frightened'. She begins to doubt her sanity too. 'You're trying to drive me out of my mind . . .' she shrieks at Charles, holding on to her senses by seeing it as 'a trick' of Charles's. In her panic, Ruth also denies Elvira's identity. 'Charles – this is madness – sheer madness – it's some sort of auto-suggestion . . .' The suggestion of being bogus sends Elvira into a rage. Unconstrained like the two suffering human beings trying to cope with her, Elvira immediately asserts herself. 'Hypnotism my foot!' she says, shattering a vase on the mantelpiece. The gesture has its calculated effect. The husband and now the wife are convinced they're going crazy.

124

The curtain comes down on Act Two Scene 1 with an image of total panic. 'Ruth gives a scream and goes into violent hysterics as the CURTAIN FALLS.'

By the next scene (2,ii) the ghost is a fact of the Condomine's life. Ruth summons Madame Arcati to exorcize Elvira. Madame Arcati is thrilled by the news of the materialization, and Ruth is suitably outraged. 'It's outrageous,' she says, when Madame Arcati can't promise to get rid of her. 'I ought to hand you over to the police. Do you realize what your insane amateur muddling has done?' Madame Arcati bridles at the word 'amateur' ('Amateur is a word I cannot tolerate' she says grandly). Ruth gets progressively more high-handed and unpleasant. 'You are entirely to blame for the whole situation,' she says before revealing to Madame Arcati that Charles only wanted 'to make notes on some of the tricks of the trade'. By refusing to help banish the ghost while gravely denouncing 'the spirit of ribaldry' in which it was invoked, Madame Arcati multiplies the fun. Ruth's fate seems sealed.

Ruth has been forced into a psychic ménage-à-trois. She's displeased at the prospect; but Charles likes the idea of being 'a kind of astral bigamist'. He keeps counselling acceptance. 'If only you'd make an effort and try to be a little more friendly to Elvira,' he tells Ruth, 'we might all have quite a jolly time'. He goes on at Ruth about what a 'unique' experience it is and how much 'fun' they could have.

RUTH: Fun! Charles – how can you – you must be out of your mind!

CHARLES: Not at all – I thought I was at first – but now I must say I'm beginning to enjoy myself.

Ruth is now as haunted by Elvira as Charles is. She is also forced to be as self-conscious. 'I've been making polite conversation all through dinner last night and breakfast and lunch today – and it's been a nightmare – and I'm not going to do it any more ...' Elvira misses no chance to make herself look like a much more appealing option than Ruth:

ELVIRA: Temper again – my poor Charles, what a terrible life
you must lead.

CHARLES: Do shut up, darling, you'll only make everything
worse.

RUTH: Who was that 'darling' addressed to – her or me?

CHARLES: Both of you.

Charles wants both of them; and Ruth can't stand the
notion of being shared. She exits leaving Elvira and Charles
alone together. When all three were on stage, Elvira made
no qualms about her affection for Charles. Amidst Ruth's
tirades, Elvira remained kittenish ('I came because the power
of Charles's love tugged and tugged and tugged at me.
Didn't it, my sweet?'). But now with Charles to herself,
Elvira's possessiveness becomes as obvious as Ruth's in Act
One. Coward reverses the symmetry. 'Do you love her?'
Elvira asks. 'As much as you loved me?' She wants to be
alone with Charles who calls her 'incorrigibly selfish'.
Finally, she relents and lets Charles go upstairs to Ruth. In
her words is a hint of tyranny: 'I'll let you go up just for a
little while if you really think it's your duty.'

By the last scene (2,iii), Elvira's tyrannical passion is destroying the household. The cook has been driven out; Edith
has a concussion; and Charles has hurt his arm in a mysteri-
ous fall. When Elvira first speaks to Charles in this scene,
her tone is completely different from the previous one. There
is a sense of petulance and domination in her voice. 'I can't
stand another of those dreary evenings at home, Charles,'
she says, insisting on a trip to the cinema in Folkestone. 'It'll
drive me dotty . . .' Charles dismisses Elvira's bad behaviour
(she throws a flower at Ruth, then leaves) as 'high spirits'.
He is still inclined to rationalize his affection for her. 'As far
as I can see the position is just as difficult for Elvira as it is
for you . . . The poor little thing comes back trustingly after
all those years in the other world and what is she faced with?
Nothing but bawling and hostility!' Coward manipulates his
plot with an expert understanding of comic hostility. Elvira

126

has clearly been creating havoc; and Ruth explains the tactic. 'It is to get you to herself for ever'. Everything points to murder. 'If you were dead', Ruth tells Charles, 'it would be her final triumph over me. She'd have you with her for ever on her damned astral plane . . .' In that moment, aware for the first time of the punishing nature of his erotic infatuation, Charles's affections swing from Elvira back to Ruth:

CHARLES: I grant you that as a character she was always rather light and irresponsible but I would never have believed her capable of low cunning . . .
RUTH: Perhaps the spirit world has deteriorated her.
CHARLES: Oh Ruth!
RUTH: For heaven's sake stop looking like a wounded spaniel and concentrate – this is serious.

Ruth rushes off to get Madame Arcati, taking the car that is supposed to drive Charles and Elvira to the cinema. The emotional and structural balance of the play is reversed. Now it is Ruth and Charles that have a secret ('I'll be back in half an hour – tell Elvira I've gone to see the vicar . . .' etc.); and now Charles finds himself defending Ruth to Elvira instead of Elvira to Ruth:

ELVIRA: Oh, Charles – have you been beastly to her?
CHARLES: No – Ruth doesn't like being thwarted any more than you do.
ELVIRA: She's a woman of sterling character. It's a pity she's so ungiving.
CHARLES: As I told you before – I would rather not discuss Ruth with you – it makes me uncomfortable.

They continue to bicker: Charles stalling for time, Elvira trying to chivvy him along to the cinema. Charles puts a stop to Elvira's petulance by announcing that they'll have to wait until Ruth returns with the car. At that, Elvira's charm disappears. She begins to act as if she too is haunted. She becomes 'agitated', then 'hysterical' and finally 'howls like a banshee'. 'What did you do?' Charles demands, fearing

127

that Elvira did want to kill him. The telephone rings, announcing a car crash and preventing a satisfactory explanation. The moment is chilling. For a second death casts a pall over the light comedy, only to mock itself. As Charles puts down the telephone, Elvira is backing away from the door 'obviously retreating from someone.'

ELVIRA: Well, of all the filthy low-down tricks. (*She shields her head with her hands and screams*). Ow – stop it – Ruth – leave go –

She runs out of the room and slams the door. It opens again immediately and slams again. CHARLES *stares aghast.*

CURTAIN

Coward's theatrical fillip is brilliant. As the door closes twice, Charles realizes that Ruth's ghost is also in the house. The whole comic premise of the play shifts. Now Elvira has landed herself with Ruth in the other world; and Charles finds himself haunted by both women. The curtain falls on a hilarious stage picture which suggests the homosexual nightmare of female suffocation.

Act Three begins with Charles in mourning; and the rest of *Blithe Spirit* deals with putting the ghosts of the dead to rest. Charles begins by getting the wayward Elvira to toe the line with Madame Arcati. He admits that he's 'perfectly furious' with Elvira and wants her dematerialized. Elvira is very much under his control. He makes her hand Madame Arcati her handbag.

ELVIRA (*picking it up and handing it to her*): Here you are.
MADAME ARCATI (*taking it and blowing her a kiss*): Oh, you darling – you little darling.

Madame Arcati's fascination is intended as a contrast with Charles's disenchantment. 'You can't expect much sympathy from me,' Charles tells Elvira when they are alone. 'I am perfectly aware that your highest hope was to murder me.' They start to quarrel. Charles is talking to a ghost from his past; and the contrary spirit won't keep quiet. Old

128

wounds still bruise them. They work themselves up into high dudgeon over the question of why Elvira went on the launch with Guy Henderson and caught the pneumonia that killed her.

ELVIRA: You seem to forget *why* I went! You seem to forget that you had spent the entire evening making sheep's eyes at that overblown harridan with the false pearls.
CHARLES: A woman in Cynthia Cheviot's position would hardly wear false pearls.
ELVIRA: They were practically all she was wearing.
CHARLES: I am pained to observe that seven years in the echoing vaults of eternity have in no way impaired your native vulgarity.

In the midst of the skirmishing, Charles calls their former marriage 'nothing but a mockery' and damns Elvira as 'feckless', 'irresponsible and morally unstable'. Elvira, for her part, tells Charles she cuckolded him on their boring honeymoon with Captain Bracegirdle. 'I was an eager young bride, Charles – I wanted glamour and music and romance', she recalls of their honeymoon. 'All I got was potted palms, seven hours every day on a damp golf course and a three-piece orchestra playing "Merrie England".' Charles counters by telling Elvira that he never wished her back alive. 'I did *not* call you back!' he says. The quarrel makes them thoroughly sick of each other. Charles asks her to go away; and she adds, 'There's nothing I should like better – I've always believed in cutting my losses. That's why I died.' Madame Arcati is called in to dematerialize Elvira. After more hilarious hocus-pocus, she manages to materialize Ruth. 'Once and for all', says Ruth, walking straight up to Charles. 'What the hell does this mean?'

Charles can't get rid of the ghosts. 'She must get you back', Charles says of Madame Arcati when Ruth complains of being messed about by her bungling. 'Anything else is unthinkable.' Having battled for possession of Charles, the two wives join forces against him:

129

ELVIRA: ... We've waited on you hand and foot – haven't we, Ruth? – you're exceedingly selfish and always were.

CHARLES: In that case I fail to see why you were both so anxious to get back to me.

RUTH: You called us back. And you've done nothing but try to get rid of us ever since we came – hasn't he, Elvira?

The wives continue to bitch Charles (RUTH: '... owing to your idiotic inefficiency, we now find ourself in the most mortifying position') and Madame Arcati (RUTH: 'If we're not careful, she'll materialize a hockey team'). Charles disclaims love for either of them, the first time in the play he admits that his show of affection hid an absence of conviction. 'Although my affection for both Elvira and Ruth is of the warmest I cannot truthfully feel that it would come under the heading that you describe', he says to Madame Arcati who is talking about Love.

'We'll win through yet – don't be downhearted,' Madame Arcati tells them all. And in the end, her faith triumphs! Edith is discovered as the natural medium who has called Elvira back and kept her there. Charles's growing mastery of his ghosts shows in his authoritative manner. He orders his wives to stand together. 'Elvira – Ruth', he commands. Ruth begins to protest, 'I resent being ordered about like this.' But Charles is firm. 'I'm afraid I must insist.' As they are sent back to the spirit world, each fires a parting salvo at Charles. Elvira confesses several indiscretions with Captain Bracegirdle, 'I couldn't have enjoyed it more' are her last unrepentant words. Ruth continues to scold Charles for his manners. 'I consider that you have behaved atrociously over the whole miserable business...'

Coward's last twist is that the ghosts have not been banished but merely rendered invisible. Madame Arcati tells Charles to 'pack your traps and go as soon as possible'. After she exits, Charles comes back into his haunted living room. He is no longer afraid of the ghosts. He has mastered them. He exults in his freedom and speaks the unspeakable.

'You said in one of your more acid moments, Ruth, that I had been hag-ridden all my life! How right you were, but now I'm free, Ruth dear, not only of Mother and Elvira and Mrs. Winthrop Llewelyn but free of you too and I should like to take this farewell opportunity of saying I'm enjoying it immensely.' The dead are laid to rest with a vengeance. 'You were very silly, Elvira, to imagine that I didn't know all about you and Captain Bracegirdle – I did. But what you didn't know was that I was extremely attached to Paula Westlake at the time!'

In admitting his sexual secrets and fear of domination, Charles displays his liberation from the ghosts. Elvira and Ruth may rattle the furniture with their tantrums, but they no longer have the power to punish him. Charles won't be ruled by old fears. 'You were becoming increasingly domineering,' he tells Ruth, doubting that his fidelity could have lasted much longer. 'And there's nothing more off-putting than that.'

Charles leaves the ghosts trapped and tormented while he exits from their havoc with perfect equanimity. 'Parting is such *sweet* sorrow' are his last teasing words to them. Charles puts guilt and the warring unseen forces that impede identity literally behind him. 'I'm going to enjoy myself as I've never enjoyed myself before,' he tells Ruth before he leaves. At the beginning of the play, Charles was a passive voyeur; at the end, he is a man of action. He assumes the ghosts' ruthlessness and their autonomy. He is full of fun. He flaunts his isolation; and in the process denies (as do all Coward's comedies) the possibility of any lasting emotional relationship. The curtain is rung down with the stage in chaos, but Charles escapes. 'He goes out of the room just as the overmantel crashes to the floor and the curtain pole comes tumbling down.' In Coward's comic world, one can emerge unscathed from the persecution of unseen forces.

Blithe Spirit is an inspired light comedy, one of the longest running plays in London theatre history (1,998 performances). Coward wanted the play to be 'very gay, superficial';[14] but the task of writing about ghosts elicited from him a more profound sense of his own hauntedness. The energy spills over into his full-bodied characters who somehow transcend Coward's boulevard decorum. No Coward comedy is better plotted, more playful or more visually inventive than *Blithe Spirit*. Its high spirits play off a very real sense of terror, sexual and otherwise. The play acts out Coward's fantasy of homosexual torment and triumph.

The ghost-like motif emerges in Coward's subsequent comedies but never in a compelling story. *Blithe Spirit* spoke to the fears of persecution, loss and death inspired by the war. 'Here we are on our little island,' Coward said in a radio pep-talk to the English in 1940. 'And the issues have become simple.'[15] But rebuilding England after the war was a complex matter. Having curried and mythologized privilege, the prospect of a democratic England put Coward's stage comedy at first on the defensive and finally on the shelf.

In *Relative Values* (1951), Coward tests one of his pet conservative theories: the fallacy of social equality. Says Crestwell the butler of Marshwood House where the haunting takes place: 'It is a social experiment based on the ancient and inaccurate assumption that, as we are all equal in the eyes of God, we should therefore be equal in the eyes of our fellow creatures.' It is a hobby-horse that lets Coward in for a very bumpy ride. In order to prove his contention, Coward contrives a situation where the old English aristocracy is about to merge with the new American meritocracy. Miranda Frayle, a British-born Hollywood celebrity whose star has lost some of its glitter, is about to marry the lord of the manor, Nigel, Earl of Marshwood. But Dora ('Moxie'), the long-time personal maid to Nigel's mother Felicity, Countess of Marshwood, can't abide the thought of Miranda Frayle becoming mistress of the house. She's adamant in her dislike and certain she'll make a bad wife. She insists on handing in her resignation. When pressed for a reason for her adamance, Dora says: 'Because she's my sister.'

In order for 'Moxie' to meet her sister on terms of complete equality, the Countess promotes her to the status of friend of the family. The sight of a servant being treated as an equal, taking meals and being on a Christian name basis with her 'masters', is the snobbism on which the joke of the play centres. But it also allows Coward to face Miranda with the ghost of her past and to examine the hauntedness in life which forces people, often against their will, to play a role. 'It is our ghosts,' Michael Goldman writes in *The Actor's Freedom*, 'all the hauntedness we carry around inside us – who make it hard for us, impossible really, to be true to ourselves, to that within which passes show.'[16] Coward understood the compulsion to 'act', and tries to dramatize it in the predicament of the sisters. 'Moxie' refuses the Countess's first notion of her posing as secretary-companion. 'This idea of play-acting and pretending to be what I'm not won't settle anything. I am what I am and I haven't got anything to be ashamed of.' Miranda, on the other hand, is all pretence. When she makes her long-awaited entrance, dressed impeccably and dutifully carrying a chintz work bag (2,i), one of her first remarks is 'What a lovely, lovely room it is. Is it haunted?' To which the Countess makes this telling reply: 'That rather depends on who occupies it.'

The room is haunted by 'Moxie'. Even before Miranda enters, Coward establishes 'Moxie's' ghost-like mission. Nigel is recounting Miranda's rags-to-riches blarney to his mother: a poor Cockney girl, a dutiful daughter until her mother died, who sought refuge from grief in America and who continued to support her drunken sister for years. Felicity knows the story is preposterous, and her words anticipate the disruption of 'Moxie's' haunting of Miranda.

FELICITY: Poor Miranda. She does seem to be haunted by intemperance, doesn't she. Is she still alive, the sister?
NIGEL: No, I don't think so.

133

FELICITY: Just as well. She might have turned up at the wedding and started throwing bottles at everybody.

'Moxie' is not only assumed dead by Nigel, she is reported dead by Miranda as she launches into the shaggy-dog story of her life. 'She died some years ago ... I hadn't heard from her in ages. I'd been sending her pennies every now and then, you know, just to help out, and food parcels and things like that, but she never acknowledged them. I'm afraid the pennies all went on drink.' 'Moxie', posing as a family guest, sits through Miranda's poised fabrications with her real identity unseen by her sister. She is a kind of living ghost. But 'Moxie' doesn't persecute Miranda immediately. She listens to the whole rewriting of their personal history, a picturesque tale that includes a childhood slum, fetching beer back from the pub for her mother, dancing to a barrel organ, and, of course, the drunken sister. The Countess knows that Miranda's real name is Freda Birch, that she was the feckless daughter of a Brixton grocer, that she scarpered from England with a showbusiness agent leaving 'Moxie' to look after their ailing mother and watch the family business go under. She also knows that Miranda 'kept on almost having babies, but not quite'. 'Moxie' is haunted by her sister's betrayal of the family; and Miranda by her guilt over the past. Miranda's own hauntedness is seen in the elaborate disguise she constructs for herself. 'I suddenly realized that for the first time in my life, I had failed, failed utterly', she says, reconstructing a mourning scene to accompany the sister's purported death. 'I felt guilty and ashamed, as though it was my fault, my responsibility. Of course it wasn't really ...' Miranda's falsification of her past shows off not her identity but her lack of it. She fears her identity and longs for it.

'Moxie', who is untouchable and invincible in the particular social sutuation, finally asserts her ghostly prerogative. She deals Miranda some rough justice. 'I wouldn't have said a word about it if you hadn't started showing off and making

134

out that you were brought up in the gutter,' 'Moxie' says, putting the *kibosh* on Nigel's wedding plans. 'Poverty and squalor indeed! A London Cockney born within the sound of Bow Bells. You were born in Number Three, Station Road, Sidcup, and if you can hear the sound of Bow Bells from Sidcup you must have the ears of an elk-hound.'

Her defences shattered, Miranda immediately 'collapses'. 'Moxie' doesn't let up. 'Moxie's' words insist on reverence for the dead and on revenge. She performs a ghostly function. 'If his Lordship takes you away and marries you three times over, it won't alter the fact that I'm your sister. You better remember that.'

'Moxie's' haunting disrupts life only to return it to the status quo. Miranda won't live with 'Moxie' or the Countess without her. So Miranda leaves, driven back into the arms of her movie star lover and her American dreams. 'Moxie' remains, secure in the bosom of her class, a happy servant to a faithful master. Coward turns the play into a feudal fairy tale. The *nouveau* world, with its ready-made identities, its hasty loyalties, and fierce insecurities, is banished; and the traditional one left intact. At the finale, Crestwell toasts the old order of things when he raises a glass to 'Moxie' and the household:

> CRESTWELL: ... I drink solemnly to you and me in our humble, but on the whole honourable calling. I drink to her Ladyship and his Lordship, groaning beneath the weight of privilege, but managing to keep their peckers up all the same. Above all I drink to the final inglorious disintegration of the most unlikely dream that ever troubled the foolish heart of man – Social Equality!

As Coward's idea of England ossified, so did his antic spirit. The hijinx and heartlessness that distinguish great comedy are the by-products of youth's fantasy of invincibility.[17] By the time of *Relative Values*, Coward was over fifty and already filled with a sense of an end. Too old now to want change in himself and to absorb the changes in English life, Coward's comic haunting of his society lost both the attack and high spirits that come with a confident sense of the world. In 1956, Coward's *Nude with Violin* launched yet another ghost into the world of modern art. But the ghost of Paul Sorodin, the dead painter, had no life or authentic mission in him. In this creaky vehicle which even Coward admitted was 'a trifle threadbare',[18] a famous artist's last will and testament announces that all his works are fake. 'My husband's insults, even beyond the grave, are powerless to hurt me,' says the great painter's last wife before the infamous letter is read aloud. It is a ghostly revenge perpetrated by the 'painter' (Paul Sorodin) 'aimed at the parasites who, in his opinion, had betrayed the only thing he really respected in human nature, the creative instinct'. Coward's argument was know-nothing, but consistent with his aversion to formlessness in art. 'I don't care what the form is,' Coward told the New York *Times*, 'as long as it is clearly defined.'[19] *Nude with Violin* was ill-defined. The ghost of Paul Sorodin dominates and torments the Estate as more letters and more painters appear threatening the market and the fame of the great dead man. But Coward can only repeat the joke, not build it to any illuminating purpose except to reiterate the reactionary whine of a man moving into old age. 'I don't think that anyone knows about painting anymore,' says Sebastien, Sorodin's former valet, his spokesman as well as Coward's. 'Art, like human nature, has got out of hand.' Coward can find no theatrical correlative to make this unseen presence effectively dramatic. The ghost is no longer a catalyst for action but for retreat. Coward's flesh was willing; but in these two plays at least, his comic spirit was weak.

5

Parting Shots

*'English drama is like the Suez Canal during Eden's war, a
means of communication made hazardous by a myriad of
sunken wrecks.'*

Kenneth Tynan, 1956

As an elder statesman of the West End, Coward was for
Tynan one of the main obstacles. 'Just above the surface, an
aluminium leviathan; the captain has not yet abandoned his
ship, on whose prow can be read the legend: "Noël Coward,
Teddington".'[1] Coward's plays were so brazenly old-
fashioned by then that they made an easy target for Tynan
and his call for a new theatre.

Coward's theatrical output after the war justified Tynan's
bitchiness. Coward's charm had long ago begun to wear thin
with the Young Turks of English theatre.[2] Coward's
boulevard theatre embodied the triumph of technique over
content against which the New Wave was rebelling.
Coward's was a theatre of enchantment; and the New Wave
wanted disenchantment. 'We need plays about cabmen and
demi-gods, plays about warriors, politicians, grocers',
wrote Tynan in 1954, surveying the parochial landscape of
English theatre. 'I counsel aggression because, as a critic,
I had rather be a war correspondent than a necrologist.'[3]

Coward's well-made plays were not always polite, but by
the fifties they seemed so. They aspired to charm, not chal-
lenge an audience. Their emphasis on balance, surface style
and formalized patterns of speech and movement eventually
robbed the plays of audacity. They could not give shape to
the upheavals of post-war English life. Coward didn't see
why they should. In the class war being waged on the English

stage, Coward fought with the old guard. The tuxedo and the teacup were his coat of arms. The Young Turks felt his plays epitomized the shrunken scope of English commercial theatre whose ambitions were as small as its accomplishments. But Coward had an actor's distrust of ideas and a faith in the potency of entertainment. An innovator in his heyday, Coward had no truck with the vaunted new demands of the English stage. 'The present cult of depression, defeatism and long-winded metaphysical philosophy arouses no interest in me, theatrically speaking,' Coward wrote. 'I am aware that two major wars are apt to upset the world's equilibrium but I still cannot quite blame the two wars for this dreadful cult of "Boredom" which seems to have the French, American and English theatre so sternly in its grip.'[4] Much of what Coward smugly dismissed as boring the intelligentsia called art. 'I've never written for the intelligentsia,' Coward said. 'Sixteen curtain calls and closed on Saturday.'[5] Coward had finally fallen out of tune with his times.

The thought had crossed Coward's mind. After the virulent critical reception in London to his best post-war play *Waiting in the Wings* (1960) and the merely moderate success of his American musical *Sail Away* (1961), Coward did some soul searching:

> Another fact that must be faced, whether I like it or not, it is perfectly possible that I am out of touch with the times. I don't care for the present trends in literature or the theatre. Pornography bores me. Squalor disgusts me. Garishness, vulgarity, and commonness of mind offend me, and problems of social significance on the stage, unless superbly well-presented, to me are a negation of entertainment. Subtlety, discretion, restraint, finesse, charm, intelligence, good manners, talent and glamour still enchant me ... Have I really or at least nearly reached the crucial moment when I should retire from the fray?[6]

Coward was embattled, but not yet convinced that his theatrical innings was over. 'I suppose it is foolish to wonder why they hate me so,' Coward wrote after *Waiting in the Wings* had been savaged by the press. 'I have been too successful for too long.'[7] He compared himself to the new playwrights and found them wanting. With the exception of Harold Pinter, the New Wave gave Coward the pip. He pronounced Beckett's *Waiting for Godot* 'pretentious rubbish without any claim to importance whatsoever'.[8] He dismissed Ionesco's *Rhinoceros* as 'a tedious play',[9] and, having read all the avant-garde in order to prep himself for his three-part diatribe against the New Wave in the *Sunday Times* (January, 1961), he concluded in his diary, 'All filled with either pretentious symbolism or violent left-wing propaganda, and none of it with any real merit.'[10] Even the works of Stanislavski came in for a private drubbing: 'soggy, pseudo-intellectual poppycock'[11] he confided to his diary. The London audience that had grown up with him had also grown old with him. As their ranks disappeared and thinned, Coward found, to his surprise, that his plays were finding no new audience. His new work could no longer be confident of long runs. His diaries gleefully record the defeats of the new movement whose temporary setbacks could not hide the fact that the tide had turned away from Coward's kind of stagecraft:

The 'new movement in the theatre' has really been taking a beating lately. The dear Royal Court produced a little number called *The Happy Haven* about an old people's home. This is performed in masks and is apparently disastrous. Miss Shelagh Delaney (*A Taste of Honey*) has produced a turkey, and that staunch upholder of the revolution, Ken Tynan, has slithered backwards off the barricades and is now enquiring rather dismally *where* all the destructiveness is leading and *what* is to be put in place of what has been destroyed! What indeed! They really are almost intolerably silly. *Nothing* has been destroyed except the enjoyment of the public and the reputations of the critics, and the former can be and is being remedied. The latter is of no consequence.[12]

In a post-war society whose priorities were being drastically overhauled, Coward was flummoxed. Frivolity, which is scepticism in cap and bells, had little to say to a society obsessed with the mission of rebuilding itself. Coward's instinct was for retreat. As the title song from *Sail Away* counselled:

> When the storm clouds are riding through a winter sky
> Sail away – sail away.

In 1956, Coward went into tax exile first in Bermuda, then in 1959 he shifted base to Switzerland. His plays too moved away from contemporary English life. Coward rejected the present. He was drawn primarily to period musicals and romantic comedies that looked to a past whose manners and meanings he could fathom and stage. These eleven post-war plays earned Coward ample bread and butter, but no glory.[13] He found himself being put critically out to pasture, not to be brought back into the fold until the mid-sixties when the National Theatre revived *Hay Fever* (1964). 'Ever since the war', he told the press, 'the critics have written me off as dead and wondered why on earth I didn't lie down. They can slam my plays as hard as they like and I shall continue trying to entertain, charm, touch and amuse the public . . .'[14]

Coward knew how to be popular, but he was no longer pertinent. The English New Wave was pertinent but would never quite learn how to be popular. The revolution in English theatre of the mid-fifties was not of form but of content. *Look Back in Anger* (1956) extended the limit of what was theatrically acceptable, just as Coward had done thirty years earlier with *The Vortex*. Speaking of Osborne and his pioneering play, Coward observed: 'We both wrote what we saw and didn't like. Mine was a more circumscribed dislike. Everything bothers him. It may be the trend of the day.'[15] It was a contentious time in which light comedy and Coward lost much of their theatrical prestige. 'There is a generation growing up', wrote the New York *Times* as

140

Coward turned sixty, 'which does not know Coward, which never knew the world he pictured and pilloried, which thinks the characters in his plays artificial and shallow.'[16] Even from his high horse, Coward couldn't conceal his bitterness at the turn of events:

> Nowadays a well-constructed play is despised and a light comedy whose only purpose is to amuse is dismissed as 'trivial' and 'without significance'. Since when has laughter been so insignificant? An actor-become-star who steps out and charms a large audience with his personality and talent is critically tolerated as though he was a performing bear. No merriment apparently must scratch the set, grim patina of these dire times . . .[17]

Coward argued with articulate naiveté for the political neutrality of entertainment. 'What neither the critics nor the contemporary pioneers take into consideration', he wrote in *The Times*, warming to the fight in 1961, 'is that political or social propaganda in the theatre, as a general rule, is a cracking bore. In spite of much wishful thinking to the contrary, the theatre is now, always has been, and I devoutly hope, always will be, primarily a place of entertainment.'[18]

But entertainment is not politically neutral. Certainly Coward's isn't. He saw theatre as a 'house of strange enchantments, a temple of illusions';[19] and the lightness of his late plays and the tone of his humour promoted this notion of escape. In so far as 'enchantment' generates a passive, uncritical, gullible public, it serves the *status quo*. Coward's late work aggressively trivializes the major aesthetic and social shifts of his day. *Nude with Violin* (1956) treats modern art as just a con. At a time when England was divesting herself of her colonial interests, Coward's *South Sea Bubble* (1950) is an imperialist fantasy in which a colony eschews independence and reform. 'Believe me', says the island potentate, cheering on imperialism. 'We are too young yet for such brave experiments. Too young and gay and irresponsible to be able to do without our Nanny.' And on the issue of democracy, *Relative Values* jokes staunchly for the *status quo ante*. 'Class', says Crestwell, with fluting irony. 'Oh dear,

141

I've forgotten what the word means.' When 'Moxie' reminds him, he says: 'It proves that you have wilfully deafened yourself to the clarion call of progress'.

Coward was a stylist confronted by a New Wave whose style was flamboyantly anti-style. Coward mourned the absence of elegance in acting and playwrighting. In his frustration, he began to sound like Eliot's Gus the Theatre Cat for whom the only great theatre was the old theatre. 'The fact that wit, charm, and elegance have been forced into temporary eclipse by our present day directors and critics, many of whom would be incapable of recognizing these qualities if they saw them, does not mean that they will not return', Coward bristled, characterizing the new kind of performance as the 'scratch and mumble school'. 'The wind and weather change; they always do.'[20]

Elegance was an adjunct of charm, a crucial part of a star's potent magic to reassure the public and keep it spellbound. In repudiating elegance, the New Wave also challenged the ideological assumptions about restraint and manners that lay beneath it. 'I'm really very tired with the whole left-wing lot,' Coward said, not putting too fine a point on it. 'They're so dreadfully scruffy. I remember the excitement of driving up to rehearsal in my best suit. Now they start rehearsing with their hands in their pockets. There is far too much grubbiness about. The theatre should dictate taste to the public, not vice-versa.'[21] In 1941, when *Blithe Spirit* received a few catcalls of 'Rubbish!' and 'Why should he get away with it!', the barracking was quickly silenced by the opening night audience. But nobody silenced the jeers at the opening of *Ace of Clubs* (1950). Coward now found himself lambasted for the rarefied world he'd been mythologizing for generations on stage. High comedy with its class nuances was becoming a genre of the past. 'There's always room for low-life plays, but the attitude that you can only have a good play if it's about people dying in dustbins is absurd', Coward wrote. 'Duchesses are quite capable of suffering.'[22] His diatribe against the New Wave was met by Tynan with showy

142

derision. 'The bridge of a sinking ship, one feels, is scarcely the ideal place from which to deliver a lecture on the technique of keeping afloat.'[23] (Ironically, it was Tynan and not Lord Olivier who a decade later pressed for the National to do *Hay Fever*.)

Having capitalized on and promoted snobbery, Coward was now victimized by what he called 'inverse snobbery'.[24] As a star, Coward believed in the uncommon man. Stardom itself was the quintessence of individualism's credo of pluck 'n luck. 'I am quite prepared to admit that during my fifty-odd years of theatre-going, I have on many occasions been profoundly moved by plays about the Common Man, as in my fifty-odd years of restaurant going I have frequently enjoyed tripe and onions, but I am not prepared to admit that an exclusive diet of either would be entirely satisfying. I am fully convinced that the general public is in complete agreement with me.'[25] To a commercial playwright, the final arbiter of taste is the box office. Coward argued that 'a glance at the list of currently successful plays in London will show that the public on the whole prefer to see extraordinary people on the stage rather than ordinary ones; fantastic situations rather than familiar, commonplace ones and actors of outsize personality and talent rather than accurately competent mediocrities.'[26]

Coward's blasts and benedictions on the theatre were consolidated most powerfully in *Waiting in the Wings* (1960), a play about retired actresses living in a charity home called 'The Wings'. 'It differs from other organizations of its kind', Coward writes in his production note, 'in that it provides only for those who have been stars or leading ladies and who, through age, lack of providence, misfortune etc., have been reduced to poverty.'[27] Coward was well-off and still in demand; but the pathos of the actresses' situation provided a resonant metaphor for his own fears of ageing and of being put artistically out to pasture. 'I really do seem to be without honour in my own country so far as the critics

143

are concerned', he wrote in his diary in 1961. 'I believe that if I turned out a real masterpiece it would still be patronized and damned with faint praise.'[28] *Waiting in the Wings* was no masterpiece, but it was his most powerful and passionate post-war play. 'I am very proud of myself because I have reconstructed *Waiting in the Wings* satisfactorily', Coward wrote in his diary on 22 April 1960. 'It is now a strong, well-constructed play and if the critics don't like it they can stuff it.'[29] It was also Coward's fiftieth produced work.

The notion of stars being forgotten, of performers' 'magic' no longer able to protect them from the vagaries of life touched something deep in Coward. It was his way of imagining an ending. The actresses – a cast which included Dame Sybil Thorndike, Marie Lohr and a number of well-known old English troupers – brought to the stage the veteran performer's indomitable spirit. The poignance of old performers, the combination of vanity and terror they hide behind their professional veneer of good cheer, is always potent stuff. The play refers to the assembled actresses as 'old shadows'; and in the opening seconds, a character twice alludes to the residents as 'a bunch of old has-beens'. The sense of their glorious past and their threadbare future weighs heavily on them and on the stage action. Coward too felt forgotten. He was still working, still in the public eye, but not in the public consciousness. When his essays on the New Wave appeared in the *Sunday Times*, he noted the public outcry in his diaries. '... One lady called Pamela Platt wrote that I should realise that my career was over and that it was unkind of the S.T. to allow "the silly old man to make such a spectacle of himself".'[30]

The actresses at 'The Wings' are completely out of the limelight. Once stars who epitomized momentum and possibility, they are now stalled and inert, waiting for the end. But the bravery that made them outstanding performers is still apparent in the good show they put on as they live out the boredom of their last years. They joke directly around

144

the point with the former actor, Perry Lasco, who is secretary to The Wings Fund:

> PERRY: That's quite usual, isn't it? I mean when people get old they can recall, say, Queen Victoria's Jubilee, and not be able to remember what happened last week.
> CORA: Nothing did.

Coward's dialogue moves with affectionate accuracy among the actresses' sense of decline and their punishing memories of stage triumphs. Once beautiful and enchanting, the loss of their spell only multiplies their impotence. The spirit in these old girls is still strong; but Nature defeats them.

> MAUDIE: Who was it that said there was something beautiful about growing old?
> BONITA: Whoever it was, I have news for him.
> ESTELLE: Since I've been here I somehow can't remember not being old.
> BONITA: Perhaps that's something to do with having played character parts for so long.
> ESTELLE: I was an ingénue for years. I was very very pretty and my eyes were enormous. They're quite small now.

To lose stardom is not only to become anonymous but to lose the aura, the 'magic', which cushions the famous. Coward was a great believer in that 'magic' both on stage and off it. These actresses, who have lost both their fame and their fortunes, have no way of manipulating experience to their advantage. Their life is controlled by the whims of others, namely The Wings Committee who oversee the maintenance of the home. Coward dramatizes this impotence. The group wants a solarium lounge so they can live out their days in the sunlight if not the limelight. The cost is £2,500: a sum which in the old days was chump change but now is exorbitant. Their request is turned down by The Wings Committee, which is run by working (and famous) actresses. The culprit is a star called Boodie Nethersole. 'I'd like to strangle her' says Cora. 'She has no right to be on the committee anyhow, she can't act her way out of a paperbag and never could.' To these old dears standards have declined; but so too have their circumstances. They have to accept what they are given, and like it. The situation is not an easy one; and the drama of this shift from glorious promise to sad resignation is elaborated after the group disappointment when Lotta Bainbridge arrives to take up residence. Renowned in youth and dignified in old age, Lotta arrives with her tearful loyal maid, Dora, whom she can no longer afford to maintain. She is Coward's model of good manners, keeping a tight reign on her emotions and bravely being civil about May Davenport, her arch enemy, who is already a fixture at 'The Wings'. 'The situation is not without humour', Lotta says with some grace. 'It is certainly ironic that Fate should arrange so neatly for May and me to end our days under the same roof. Personally I can't help seeing the funny side of it, but I doubt that May does.'

The feud between Lotta and May and the question of the solarium dominate *Waiting in the Wings*. By Act One Scene Two Lotta is familiar with the residents and the routine – a regimen filled with the spirited antics of the bombastic Deirdre O'Malley and the senile ramblings of Sarita Myrtle who comes down the staircase in a nightgown complaining of chill one second and reciting Shakespeare the next.

SARITA: Out, damned spot! Out I say! One two: why then, 'tis time to do't.
MISS ARCHIE (*firmly*). You must *not* quote Macbeth in this house, Miss Myrtle. You know how it upsets everybody.

Death is what's really waiting in the wings; and Lotta, Coward's spokesman for 'good form', sensibly faces up to the hard facts of life. Coward himself refused to get sullen over his intimations of mortality. 'I'll settle without apprehension for oblivion', he wrote in his diary. 'I cannot really feel that oblivion will be disappointing. Life and love and fame and fortune can all be disappointing, but not dear old

146

oblivion. Hurrah for eternity.'[31] Lotta may not have Coward's good cheer but she has his good manners. She makes a case for them when she intercedes in a quarrel between Deirdre and the vain May Davenport. May tells her to mind her own business, and Lotta quickly replies: 'It's the business of all of us in this house to live together as amicably as possible without causing each other any embarrassment.' Later in the scene when she holds out a hand of friendship that is at first refused, Lotta tells May, 'We had better face one harsh fact, May. We have fallen on evil days and there is no sense in making them more evil than they need be. We haven't many years left, and very, very little to look forward to. Let's for God's sake forget the past and welcome our limited future with as much grace as possible.'

Lotta's credo expresses in private terms the aesthetic behind Coward's notion of public entertainment. Manners insist on a truce with reality, creating harmony by avoiding embarrassment. 'Taste may be vulgar', Coward said. 'But it must never be embarrassing. There is no need to embarrass anyone.'[32] Lotta wants to manufacture an illusion of well-being just as Coward's theatre wants to create a sense of reassurance. For Lotta and for Coward, vulgarity and contentiousness are the enemies of order; and a show of duty and reasonableness are what sustain and enhance the social fabric. Both Lotta and Coward define as good what puts their society at ease. Both insist that life is to be enjoyed and that pleasure is the fruit of discipline. On this point, Coward was adamant. 'I believe whole-heartedly in pleasure. As much pleasure as possible and as much work. I am very light-minded and very serious. I have no religion, but I believe in courage. I loathe fear and cruelty and hatred and destructiveness . . .' The taste, elegance, clarity and narrative balance Coward demanded in theatre was the stage equivalent to the carapace of optimism he wore in life. Even when examining old age and death, Coward refuses death its dominion. 'The play as a whole contains the basic truth', Coward wrote in his introduction, 'that old age needn't be nearly so dreary and sad as it is supposed to be, provided you greet it with humour, and live it with courage.'[33]

To Coward, politeness was a form of courage. In theatrical terms, Coward saw it as also good business. *Waiting in the Wings* was Coward's tasteful answer to the nihilism, self-pity and crass excess he saw in the New Wave. 'It is true that a writer should hold a mirror up to nature, although there are certain aspects of nature which would be better unreflected', Coward wrote, listing various acts of defecation, urination and labour pains he'd seen on stage. 'Now in my experience an audience is quite prepared to have its susceptibilities shocked from time to time and frequently enjoys it but ... and it is a very big but – only up to a point. Once that point is reached and passed, the audience, who has paid its money into the box-office in order to be entertained, stimulated or moved, rebels. Its rebellion is passive and unsensational. It just stays away ...'[34]

In the Lotta-May feud, Coward puts the issue of politeness centre stage. *Waiting in the Wings* acts out the triumph of good manners. By Act Two Scene Two, Lotta and May have made up their quarrel of thirty years. They are no longer divided by the past but united by their present plight. 'I consider the reconciliation between Lotta and May in Act Two Scene Two and the meeting between Lotta and her son in Act Three Scene Two, are two of the best scenes I have ever written', Coward said, in his special pleading for the play in *Play Parade 6*.[35] What both scenes slickly dramatize is reason politely containing and transforming hostile emotion. 'Why did you take him from me?' May asks Lotta about her husband Charles, only to learn that he'd had another mistress on the rebound from May. Lotta's reasonableness defuses the situation and prevents emotion from spilling over into 'vulgar' recrimination:

LOTTA: ... Charles fell in love with me and I fell in love with him and we were married. I have no regrets.

MAY (*drily*): You are very fortunate. I have, a great many.

LOTTA: Well, don't. It's a waste of time.

By the end of the scene, they are raising their glasses of whisky to each other in a ritual of civility. 'Well, Lotta', May says, rising and holding up her glass. 'We meet again'. They echo the ironic toast of *This Happy Breed*. 'Happy days!' they say to each other as the curtain falls.

Coward staunchly believed in not breaking faith with the public. 'To my mind one of the principle faults of the "New Movement" writers is their supercilious attitude to the requirements of average audience', he wrote, giving a little boulevard advice to the new generation. 'Consider the public. Treat it with tact and courtesy ...'[36] *Waiting in the Wings* also dramatizes this issue of breaking faith when a well-known tabloid journalist, prepared to make a TV appeal for the Wings solarium in exchange for a feature story, is set among them by Perry. The plot point may be pat; but it serves to dramatize yet another aspect of Coward's vision of good manners: loyalty. Passing herself off under a pseudonym, Zelda infiltrates the home. She meets Osgood Meeker. A model of loyalty, Meeker is a seventy-year-old fan who still pays homage each week to one of the nonagenarians in residence. 'She hadn't much of anything', Osgood says, remembering Miss Carrington on the music hall stage. 'Except magic, but she had a great deal of that.' When Zelda encounters the gaga Sarita Myrtle, Coward contrives a funny and poignant exchange that catches the sweet obsession of a performer's life:

ZELDA: It's a very nice house, isn't it?
SARITA: Capacity.

Zelda Fenwick's cover is blown by Lotta who recognizes her from the logo of her column. Although Perry and Zelda have colluded in the name of a good cause, they have broken faith with the group and with the rules of the home. Many of the actresses are outraged; and Lotta tries to reason Zelda out of writing the story. She pitches her appeal on the grounds of loyalty both to the actresses' dignity and the memory of the public who've enjoyed them. 'The last thing we want any more is publicity', she explains, in vain. 'It would shed too harsh a light on us, show up lines and wrinkles, betray to the world how old and tired we are. That would be an unkind thing to do. We are still actresses in our hearts, we still have our little vanities and prides. We'd like to be remembered as we were, not as we are ...'

Despite her plea, the article is written; and it turns out to be the story of the Lotta-May feud which has subsequently been patched up. Lotta laughs off the sloppy sensationalism, but May remains furious. She echoes the burden of Coward's song: 'I'm thankful I'm old and near the end of my time. All the standards are lowered, all the values have changed. There is no elegance, dignity or reticence left.' But Coward, who contrived a persona that was above bitterness and rancour, is shrewd enough theatrically not to button-hole an audience. He undercuts May's remark with mockery. One of the old dears gets to the piano (they always do in a Coward play) and sings:

Waiting in the Wings – Waiting in the Wings –
'Older than God, On we plod
Waiting in the Wings' –

After Sarita Myrtle has inadvertently set fire to her room, she is escorted from 'The Wings' to a hospital by a young doctor (2,iii), an exit reminiscent of Blanche Dubois' in *A Streetcar Named Desire*. As always in Coward's theatre, the tragic scene is played not for pain but for sentiment. '*Au revoir*, my dears', Sarita says, turning at the door before she exits. 'It has been such a really lovely engagement. Good luck to you all.' In this expert piece of stage engineering, the moment is effective without being unnerving: a combination which is Coward's recipe for commercial success.

In Act Three, the loss and death that haunt 'The Wings' finally coalesce. Coward counterpoints the melancholy with songs and other displays of hope. Zelda Fenwick's editor makes a personal gift of the solarium; and Zelda herself brings champagne to the ladies as a gesture of apology. In

150

the midst of the merry-making, the dance in old Deirdre finally gives out. 'Mother of God, it's happening', she says, in a powerful line. 'It's happening to me – it's happening – to me –'. The curtain comes down on 3,i with May folding Deirdre's dead hands over her breast, and saying bitterly, 'The luck of the Irish!'

May cannot accept her condition; but Lotta does. Lotta sends away her son who has returned after an absence of thirty years to ask her to live with him and his family in Canada. 'This is a dreadfully difficult moment Alan – full of sadness and regret and a sort of hopelessness. I can't find any words to describe it', Lotta says, finding the words. '... I'm merely trying to make you see that certain gestures in life are irrevocable.' Resigned to her life ('I am resigned, you see, and finally content', Lotta tells May in 3,ii), Lotta rejects change and accepts her situation. With a great show of decorum, she sends her son away.

The play ends with a terrific final curtain that captures the spirited decency and bittersweet irony of the old troupers. Topsy Baskerville, a musical comedy star during World War 1, is coming to 'The Wings' to fill the place left by Deirdre O'Malley. The old girls remember her at the height of her fame in 1915, and Mandie sings her trade-mark 'Oh Mr. Kaiser'. The song is a youthful, impudent number:

Oh Mr. Kaiser
Call your legal adviser
You've bitten off far more than you can chew
When Mister Tommy Atkins comes a-marching to Berlin
You'll be gibbering like a monkey in the zoo
(Have a banana!)

But when Topsy appears, she is 'a small, frail old lady in her seventies'. Coward's stage picture relishes the sentiment of the moment. As she enters, Topsy hears 'Oh Mr. Kaiser' being played on the piano. 'My song!' she exclaims in a tremulous voice. The curtain falls with the entire cast

151

singing Topsy's old, defiant refrain which, then as now, inspires courage in the face of death.

In the jaunty, moving finale Coward's love of the theatre and of the generosity of theatre folk is forcefully stated. *Waiting in the Wings* is unusual in the Coward canon for the depth, directness and intensity of its feeling. At the finale, the old troupers display the resilience and hopefulness Coward associated with performing. Judging by the reception of the first night London audience, Coward's instincts about drama and audiences seemed to be right on target. 'At the end, there was a really tremendous ovation', Coward wrote in his diary on 11 September 1960. 'And when I finally emerged from the theatre an hour later, there were cheering crowds on both sides of St. Martin's Lane.'[37]

But the press had no public triumph to report the next day. The headlines were as vicious as the reviews: JUST TIMELESS-ROOTLESS PRATTLE; NOËL'S DULL 50th; FIRST NIGHT-MARE. 'To read them', Coward wrote in his diary, 'was like being repeatedly slashed in the face. I don't remember such concentrated venom for many a long day.'[38]

'If at this late stage of my life I were to have another series of resounding failures I believe I could regard them with a certain equanimity',[39] Coward had told the New York *Times* in 1960 on the occasion of his sixtieth birthday. The reception of *Waiting in the Wings* was the acid test of this boast, and Coward failed it. He was hurt and bewildered by the viciousness of the critical response. There was nothing calm about Coward's reply to his critics over the play. 'Let them reserve their raves for those dreary little experimental plays that only they can understand and nobody goes to see unless he wants to be bored to death', he fumed to the *Daily Mail*.[40] His words were unworthy of him. *Waiting in the Wings* closed in London after a four month run but eked out another five months on tour. Its commercial and critical failure was a blow to Coward. The play was much better than the critics' response to it; but its sedate form was passé.

152

Coward felt 'time's winged chariot goosing me',[41] but his plays, if not his cabaret performance, had long ago lost the energy to goose the audience. Vivacity was absent from his stage pictures and from his stage language. And the new writers – whatever Coward's questionable assessment of their merits – brought to their plays an ambitiousness of design, a linguistic nuance that made the body of Coward's popular oeuvre appear at once less awesome and accomplished.

Coward's reactionary position became entrenched over the next few years. His argument about elegance failed to appreciate the stylistic advances of the New Wave. His caterwauling about manners missed the point that bad manners are manners too. From his catbird seat in Switzerland, he couldn't hear the brutality in his showy optimism.

Well, I was getting awfully sick of this emphasis on the under-privileged and proletariat on account of it being entirely a mis-representation of fact [Coward said in 1964, explaining his reasons for attacking the modern theatre scene]. No people in the world have a better time than the English. If you go round a few pubs in the East End or Chelsea, or anywhere you like, they have a ball. They come around and scream and enjoy themselves, and then we go to the Royal Court Theatre and we see people who lack communication with each other, who are miserable, who are trying to break through this terrible social barrier – they don't do any such thing. They're as merry as grigs, all of them. Obviously there is a certain amount of poverty and disease and unhappiness but not nearly as much as in other countries. The Welfare State is doing very nicely, thank you.[42]

Although Coward continued to slag the Royal Court, he'd joined its bandwagon in 1959. His *Look after Lulu*, an adaptation of Feydeau's *Occupe-toi d'Amélie* which starred Vivien Leigh, played to 97% capacity at the Royal Court; and then transferred to the West End where it did not find such favour. And in 1966 at a gala performance of Arnold

Wesker's *The Kitchen* to raise money for the George Devine Award, a playwrighting prize that encouraged the kind of theatre he so thoroughly despised, Coward played the Maitre D. At the end of his career, as at its beginning, Coward had the star's itch to be where the action was. While the decade's spirit of bumptious liberation could never infiltrate far into his art, Coward gamely tried to move with the times. He lectured a generation he couldn't influence, only to have it influence him. In 1965, returning to the West End for the first time since 1953, Coward starred in his newest play, *A Song at Twilight*, played in alternating repertoire with *Shadows of the Evening* and *Come into the Garden Maud*. They were given the omnibus title, *Suite in Three Keys*. The longest and best play was *A Song at Twilight*, about a world-famous writer being forced to face up to the hypocrisy of his homosexuality in his life and his work. Inspired by and looking like Somerset Maugham, Coward acted out his own obsession with reputation and the creative price he'd had to pay for a lifetime of subterfuge. As Hugo Latymer, Coward was still putting on a masquerade; but he was bravely trying to open a few cracks in the facade. In the brazen mood of the sixties, there was no need for frivolity's disguise; and Coward's grave attempt at the provocative signalled the professional entertainer's instinct for meeting the demands of a new generation of theatre-goers. His straight-talking about homosexuality – the issue disguised as drug-taking in *The Vortex* and the code behind the frivolity in his great comedies – was as far as he could go toward dropping his legendary reticence.

'Homosexuality is becoming as normal as blueberry pie.'[43] In his diary, Coward ruminated on the new atmosphere of sexual freedom and how it could have affected his earlier work in which he invented a heterosexual posture for himself that evaded the emotional issues of his life. He was inured to the frankness of a new generation. 'Ah me! The ladies. God bless 'em', he went on in his diary. 'What silly cunts they make themselves. It's quite all right to say cunt now because the Lady Chatterley case has been won, and already fuck, balls, arse and shit have been printed on the second page of the *Observer* and the *Spectator*. Hurrah for free speech and the death of literature.'[44] Coward could best tease the issue of sexuality in song where his safety was in his speed. In 'Spinning Song', he imagines himself at the spinning wheel:

> My bobbin goes click-clack, click-clack,
> I've got my warp right up my woof
> And I can't get the bloody thing back.

But in his plays, Coward had masked his deepest feelings. Coward's quarrelling heterosexual couples rationalized his predicament: a universe where people found it impossible to live apart or together. He memorialized his own isolation in 'I Travel Alone':

> When the dream is ended and passion has flown
> I travel alone.
> Free from love's illusion, my heart is my own:
> I travel alone.

A Song at Twilight faces the punishing dilemma of keeping up heterosexual appearances. Hugo Latymer's life is built around sustaining his eminent reputation. When the curtain comes up, Hilde, his wife of twenty-four years, is insisting on Hugo's right to veto the script and the adaptor of one of his novels for the movies. 'I think it matters a great deal', she says. 'It involves his name and reputation.' Hilde is part of Latymer's carapace of success. She protects both his interests and his image. Into this scene of literary eminence, Coward introduces Carlotta Gray, a woman with whom Latymer long ago had a two-year affair. She greets Hilde with a mischievous compliment about the nerve-racking business of living with a man of such prestige. 'The continual demands made upon his time, the constant strain of having to live up to the self-created image he has implanted in the public mind. How fortunate he is to have you to protect him.' When they are alone, Carlotta returns to her theme of Latymer's wonderful career. 'At least you can congratulate yourself, on having had a fabulously successful career. How wonderful to have been able to entertain and amuse so many millions of people for such a long time. No wonder you got a Knighthood.' But there is a nervy edge to Carlotta's comments. After all these years, she still smarts from the way Latymer exploited, then dispatched her from his life. He had hoped to be greeting a friend; and he rightly suspects he is facing an enemy. Carlotta has come with a purpose; and at first, her mission isn't altogether clear. 'Your book', she says, speaking of Latymer's autobiography, 'may have been an assessment of the outward experience of your life, but I cannot feel that you were entirely honest about your inner ones.' She is charming and truculent; he alternates between the waspish and the benign. Act One is a fencing match between them, in which their pasts, their careers, their passage into old age is discussed. Finally, over dinner, she mentions that she has written her autobiography and asks permission to publish his letters. Latymer firmly refuses. 'You may have them if you like', she says, returning to the subject of the letters as she prepares to leave. 'They are of no further use to me . . . I'm afraid I can't let you have the others though . . .' The other letters are to Perry Sheldon.

HUGO: What do you know about Perry Sheldon?
CARLOTTA: Among other things that he was the only true love of your life. Goodnight, Hugo. Sleep well.

And on that melodramatic revelation, the curtain falls on Act 1.

Carlotta is contemplating turning the letters over to Latymer's biographer. She isn't sure what to do with them. 'They were written', she tells Hugo in Act Two, 'in your earlier years . . . before your mind had become corrupted by fame and your heart by caution.' She goes on at him about his 'carefully sculptured reputation', the 'ceaseless vigilance (of) your "bubble reputation".' The battle is now joined.

Carlotta is not trying to blackmail Latymer, but to force him to admit his hypocrisy. Even when cornered, Latymer hides from his true self.

> HUGO: ... The veiled threat is perfectly clear ... The threat to expose to the world the fact that I have had, in the past, homosexual tendencies.
> CARLOTTA (*calmly*): Homosexual tendencies in the past! What nonsense! You've been a homosexual all your life, and you know it!

The skirmishing continues, with the argument about homosexuality coming as close to his own knuckle as Coward ever allowed.

> HUGO: According to the law in England, homosexuality is still a penal offence.
> CARLOTTA: In the light of modern psychiatry and in the opinion of all sensible and unprejudiced people that law has become archaic and nonsensical.
> HUGO: Nevertheless it exists.
> CARLOTTA: It won't exist much longer.
> HUGO: Maybe so, but even when the actual law ceases to exist there will still be a stigma attached to 'the love that dare not speak its name' in the minds of millions of people for generations to come ...
> CARLOTTA: Do you seriously believe that now, today, in the middle of the Twentieth century, the sales of your books would diminish if the reading public discovered that you were sexually abnormal?
> HUGO: My private inclinations are not the concern of the reading public. I have no urge to martyr my reputation for the sake of self-indulgent exhibitionism.
> CARLOTTA: Even that might be better than vitiating your considerable talent by dishonesty.
> HUGO: Dishonesty? In what way have I been dishonest.'
> CARLOTTA: Subtly in all your novels and stories but

> quite obviously in your autobiography ... But why the con-
> stant implications of heterosexual ardour? Why those self-
> conscious, almost lascivious references to laughing-eyed dam-
> sels with scarlet lips and pointed breasts? ...

Coward too had steadfastly dodged the issue of homosexuality in his writing. He had posed as a romantic comedian and turned his fantasy of heterosexual conquest into
show-biz legend. Instead of being explorations of consciousness, the majority of his plays remained exploitations of his
self-consciousness. Popularity only intensified the masquerade. His burnished charm won him a wide following, but
trapped him in a perpetual star performance. He rationalized this alienation as duty. 'If you're a star, you have to
behave like one', he told the New York *Times*. 'The public
are very demanding. They have a right to be ...'[45]

Latymer, like Coward, had sacrificed much of his inner
life to public reputation. When Carlotta takes Latymer to
task for his lack of moral courage and fundamental dis-
honesty, there is no real comeback. 'You might have been a
great writer instead of merely a successful one', she says, a
mouthpiece for Coward's autumnal thoughts. 'And you
might also have been a far happier man.'

Hilde, who returns a bit tipsy from dinner with a friend,
testifies to Latymer's isolation. Caught in the crossfire
between Latymer and Carlotta, she admits to having always
known about his homosexuality. 'I would have liked you to
have told me long ago, it would have shown me that even if
you didn't love me, you at least were fond enough of me to
trust me.' Carlotta points out to both of them how Hugo
has exploited her. 'You don't find it humiliating to have
been used by him for twenty years not only as an unpaid
secretary, manager and housekeeper, but as a social camouflage as well?' But Hilde is prepared to let Latymer's depend-
ence substitute for love. In the end, Carlotta relents and
gives Hugo the letters before she exits.

The play ends in a tableau of isolation and regret. Hugo
sits in his armchair scanning the letters. 'It is apparent', the

stage directions say, 'from his expression that he is deeply moved'. He starts to read the letter again and then with a sigh covers his eyes with his hand. When Hilde comes back in the room from seeing Carlotta to the door, she sits apart from Latymer on the sofa. He doesn't turn around.

HUGO (*after a long pause*): I heard you come in.
HILDE (*almost in a whisper*): Yes. I thought you did.

HUGO continues reading the letter as–
THE CURTAIN SLOWLY FALLS

Coward began and ended his career writing about charm. Hugo Latymer, as Alan Brien rightly pointed out 'is Garry Essendine thirty sapping years on ... after a lifetime of self-indulgence and self-advertisement'.[46] But whereas *Present Laughter* dramatized a predicament. *A Song at Twilight* merely states it. Coward had found neither a technical nor emotional solution to the problem he tried bravely to pose. It was as if, wrote Brien, 'the greatest theatrical entertainer of our century (was) desperately signalling to us that he has a message but is afraid he lacks the equipment to transmit it across the footlights'[47]. Coward was too much of a stranger to his intimate feelings to make his vulnerability articulate. Even his language foreshadowed a hardening of his theatrical arteries. Coward's prose, like his body, grew flabby toward the end. Hugo Latymer's world and his language had lost touch with reality, and Coward's prose is tall by walking on tiptoes. Alan Brien correctly called attention to the strut of Latymer's 'second-rate Cowardisms ... the pseudo highbrow vocabulary, full of difficult dead words like "prescience", "obloquy", "egregious", "vitiating", and "gratuitous", which sound strained and hollow. The insults are repetitive and depend on a few over-worked, italicized adverbs, such as "*interminably* witless" and "*inexpressibly* tedious".'[48] Coward's idiom only reinforced the public facade grown by now too solid to crack. Still, Coward's return to the West End was a big event; and *A Song at Twilight*, as well as the even skimpier *Shadows of the Evening* and *Come*

159

into the Garden Maud, earned Coward surprising accolades. 'I haven't experienced anything like it in many a long day', he wrote.[49]

Coward was moving from merry-andrew to museum piece. Having so well reflected aspects of his generation in his plays, his stage world came to epitomize the styles and attitudes of a time which, from the vantage point of the tumultuous sixties, seemed light years away. The Hampstead Theatre Club's revival of *Private Lives* (1963) and the National's *Hay Fever* (1964) signalled a change in Coward's theatrical fortunes. The critics' about-face on Coward in *Suite in Three Keys* was proof (if more was needed) that the tide had turned again in Coward's favour. Coward dubbed this happy state of affairs 'Dad's Renaissance'. Coward's songs, the best of which had never lost their currency, were also resurrected for a new generation of enthusiasts in the successful West End musical anthology *Cowardy Custard*. Another transatlantic show *Oh! Coward* won comparable kudos on Broadway.

When 'Destiny's Tot' became Sir Noël Coward in January 1970, his theatrical rehabilitation was complete. The knighthood coincided with a week's celebration of his talents by BBC-TV which featured various Coward plays for seven consecutive days. Coward referred to this as 'Holy Week'.

In the barrage of publicity about his life and work that followed Coward from the mid-sixties until his death on 26 March 1973, the press had difficulty separating the first-rate from the fecund-rate. The critical overkill amused even Coward:

'Do you think I'm the wittiest man alive? This paper says I am' [writes Cole Lesley, Coward's companion and biographer, in *The Life of Noël Coward*]. What could you say except, 'I suppose you must be. Who else is there? Try to name a wittier'. He would consider, 'There might be someone at this very moment being witty as all get-out in Urdu'.[50]

In print, Coward's wit was, as Tynan politely put it, 'variable'.[51] On stage, he would rarely allow himself the quicksilver displays of anger and bitchiness that could be so devastating off it. 'He began, like many other satirists (Evelyn Waugh for instance) by rebelling against conformity, and ended up by making peace with it, even becoming its outspoken advocate,'[52] wrote Tynan. When Coward's wit was youthful and combative, his comedies display the antic mischievousness that make a few of them exemplary. But when the only mission of his laughter was to curry public favour, both his wit and the theatre it served lose their excellence. Having inveighed against the avant-garde's failure to consider the public, Coward erred in the opposite direction. It is not enough to entertain people, you have to entertain ideas.

'Forty years ago', Tynan wrote when Coward was 53, 'Noël Coward was Slightly in *Peter Pan*, and you might say that he has been wholly in *Peter Pan* ever since'.[53] Coward, whose frivolity taunted death in his early plays, did so till the end. At 60, Coward was writing in his diary, 'I've had a wonderful life. I've still got rhythm, I've got music, who could ask for anything more.'[54] And at 70, his impish high-spirits were still asserting themselves, mocking the inevitable defeat of old age and living up to one of his definitions of style: 'evading boredom' –

He began to act the part of an old man before he became one, moaning 'I am old, Father William', or simulating a wheeze or a querulous croak, 'I am old, and scant of breath'. [Cole Lesley writes.] Another joke was to have to be helped out of bed because he was so frail and aged, hobbling bent double on his way to the bathroom and then executing a snappy buck-and-wing before he went inside to close the door.[55]

Coward, who was as old as the century, personified all its deliriums. His obsession with output, industry, fame, momentum, enchantment were those of modern life that his stage success made glorious. 'Really my life', he wrote, 'has

161

been one long extravaganza.'[56] An entrepreneur of expectation, Coward planned it that way. In his long span in show business, there were better songs, better plays, better music, even better comedians than Coward. But nobody succeeded in so many areas of show business at such a high level of proficiency as Coward did. 'If I had to write my own epitaph', he said, 'it would be: "He was much loved because he made people laugh and cry".'[57] But Coward's achievement was more than that. He was a phenomenon. He knew his public and articulated its dreams. His plays and songs exerted a powerful influence in shaping the society's sense of itself. In doing so, Coward also invented himself and an aristocracy of success in which to move. Coward was one of those individuals born to every era whose life and work, however uneven, are among the blueprints by which future generations reconstruct the follies and the accomplishments of times gone by.

Notes

Introduction – Impresario of Himself
1. Kenneth Tynan, *The Sound of Two Hands Clapping* (London: Jonathan Cape, 1975), p. 58.
2. As quoted in Cole Lesley, *The Life of Noël Coward* (London: Penguin Books, 1978), p. 149.
3. Sean O'Casey, *The Green Crow* (New York: George Braziller, 1956), p. 98. In 'Coward Codology: 1', O'Casey says: "The truth is, of course, that Noël Coward hasn't yet even put his nose into the front rank of second-class dramatists, let alone into the front rank of first-class dramatists".
4. Cole Lesley, *The Life of Noël Coward*, p. xvi.
5. *Ibid.*, p. 65.
6. Sheridan Morley, *A Talent to Amuse* (London: Heinemann, 1969), p. 204.
7. Kenneth Tynan, *Curtains* (London: Longmans, 1961), p. 61.
8. Morley, *A Talent to Amuse*, p. 195.
9. *Ibid.*, p. 93.
10. Sean O'Casey, *The Green Crow*, p. 112.
11. *Ibid.*, p. 92.
12. Coward, *Play Parade Vol. 4* (London: Heinemann, 1954), p. xiii.
13. Morley, *A Talent to Amuse*, p. 97.
14. Lesley, *The Life of Noël Coward*, p. 484.
15. *Ibid.*, p. 151.
16. Tynan, *The Sound of Two Hands Clapping*, p. 60.
17. Coward, 'These Old Fashioned Revolutionaries', *Sunday Times*, 15 January 1961.
18. Tynan, *The Sound of Two Hands Clapping*, p. 62.

1: The Politics of Charm

1. Dick Richards (ed.), *The Wit of Noël Coward* (London: Leslie Frewin, 1968), p. 63.
2. Edgar Lustgarten, 'Noël Coward Talks', BBC Radio, 27 January 1972.
3. As quoted in Morley, *A Talent to Amuse*, p. 85.
4. Peter Quennell, *The Wanton Chase* (London: Collins, 1980), p. 147–8.
5. Hunter Davies, "Noël Coward on Being 70", New York *Times*, December 1970.
6. 'Noël Coward on Acting', interviewed by Michael Macowan, 12 March 1966.
7. *Ibid.*
8. As quoted in Richard Buckle (ed.), *Self-Portrait with Friends*: The Selected Diaries of Cecil Beaton (London: Weidenfeld and Nicolson, 1979), p. 12.
9. *Ibid.*
10. Coward, *Present Indicative* (London: Heinemann, 1937), p. 4.
11. As quoted in Charles Castle, *Noël* (London: W. H. Allen, 1974), p. 65.
12. John Lehmann and Derek Parker (eds.), *The Letters of Edith Sitwell* (London: Macmillan, 1970), p. 29.
13. James Lees-Milne, *Prophesying Peace* (London: Chatto and Windus, 1977), p. 152.
14. As quoted in Robert Rhodes James (ed.), *Chips: The Diaries of Sir Henry Chips Channon* (London: Weidenfeld and Nicolson, 1967), pp. 412–13.
15. Coward, *Present Indicative*, p. 112.
16. *Ibid.*, p. 117.
17. Lesley, *The Life of Noël Coward*, p. 94.
18. Ronald Hayman, *Playback*, 'Interview with Noël Coward' (London: Davis-Poynter, 1973), p. 149.
19. 2 February 1923.
20. *Observer*, 5 February 1923.
21. Coward, *Present Indicative*, p. 190.
22. *Ibid.*, p. 240.

23. Hunter Davies, New York *Times*, December 1969.
24. Tynan, *Curtains*, p. 60.
25. Castle, *Noël*, p. 64.
26. *Manchester Evening News*, July 1920.
27. *The Sketch*, 1925.
28. Coward, *Play Parade Vol. 1*, p. x.
29. Coward, *Three Plays* (The Rat Trap, The Vortex and Fallen Angels): with the Author's Reply to His Critics, (London: Ernest Benn, 1925), p. vi.
30. Coward, *Evening Standard*, 31 December 1924.
31. S. P. R. Mais, *Daily Graphic*, 29 November 1924.
32. Davies, New York *Times*, December 1969.
33. Coward, *Present Indicative*, p. 229.
34. *Ibid.*, p. 229.
35. Coward, *Play Parade Vol. 2* (London: Heinemann, 1939), p. ix.
36. Lesley, *The Life of Noël Coward*, p. 116.
37. *Sunday Chronicle*, 26 April 1925.
38. Cole Lesley chronicles the real life performance this way: 'He would fling himself on to a chair or a sofa and exclaim from the depths of extreme despondency (perhaps his typewriter ribbon had buckled) "Life has dealt me another blow ..."' As quoted in *The Life of Noël Coward*, p. 100.
39. Lustgarten, 'Noël Coward Talks', BBC-Radio, 1972.
40. As quoted in Lesley, *Life of Noël Coward*, p. 122.

2: Comedies of Bad Manners
1. *Observer*, 3 April 1931.
2. A. J. P. Taylor, *English History: 1914–1945* (London, Oxford University Press, 1965), p. 302–3.
3. *Ibid.*, p. 259.
4. Coward, *Three Plays*, p. x.
5. Lustgarten, 'Noël Coward Talks', 1972.
6. Coward, *Three Plays*, p. x.
7. Taylor, *English History: 1914–45*, p. 171.

8. Somerset Maugham, *The Summing Up* (London: Heinemann, Collected Edition, 1948), p. 154–5.
9. New York *Times*, 17 December 1969.
10. Coward, *Three Plays*, p. viii.
11. *Ibid.*, x.
12. *Ibid.*, vii.
13. *Ibid.*, vii.
14. As quoted in Lesley, *The Life of Noël Coward*, p. 65.
15. As quoted in John Russell Taylor, *The Rise and Fall of the Well-Made Play* (London: Methuen, 1967), p. 134.
16. Coward, *Play Parade Vol. 2*, p. ix.
17. *Ibid.*, pp. viii–ix.
18. Maugham, *The Summing Up*, pp. 154–55.
19. *Ibid.*
20. Coward explained: 'Laurette invariably said, "Now we'll play a word game". Well, the guests shrank with horror and some poor beast had to pick up a box and put it somewhere, and Laurette would say "No, *no*! That's not the way to do it at all." So then she would do it. Beautifully. And her family and we all would all applaud, and then we'd go onto the next word. And those evenings got such a reputation for *dread* in America that hardly anyone ever went at all. And I see their point.' As quoted in Castle, *Noël*, p. 48.
21. Coward, *Present Indicative*, p. 412.
22. *Ibid.*, p. 208.
23. *Ibid.*, p. 234.
24. John Fisher, *Call Them Irreplaceable* (London: Elm Tree Books–Hamish Hamilton, 1974), p. 68.
25. Ronald Bryden, *Unfinished Hero and Other Essays* (London: Faber, 1969), p. 54.
25a. *Ibid.*, p. 53.
26. Coward, *Present Indicative*, p. 240.
27. Bryden, *Unfinished Hero*, p. 55
28. New York *Times*, December 1969.
29. *Sunday Times*, 11 June 1925.
30. As quoted in Lesley, *The Life of Noël Coward*, p. 138.

31. 'Noël Coward on Acting', BBC Radio, 12 March 1966.
32. Ivor Brown, *Week-End*, 4 October 1930.
33. Coward wrote: 'Although *Private Lives* has always been patronised by the American and English critics, it has also been enthusiastically and profitably patronised by the public wherever and in whatever language it is played'. As quoted in Noël Coward, *Future Indefinite* (London: Heinemann, 1954), p. 324.
34. Coward, *Present Indicative*, p. 373.
35. Coward, *Play Parade Vol. 2*, p. viii.
36. Coward, *Present Indicative*, pp. 375-6.
37. 'Noël Coward Talks About Acting', BBC-Radio, 12 March 1966.
38. As quoted in Lesley, *The Life of Noël Coward*, p. 155.
39. In *The Glass of Fashion* (Weidenfeld and Nicolson, 1954), Cecil Beaton writes: 'In the rise of the whole new spirit of affectation and frivolity, the influence of the theatre was far from negligible. By the later 20's young women gave up speaking in mellifluous tones in favour of cigarette-throat voices, rasping and loud. Men enjoyed imitating the exaggerated, clipped manners of certain actors and adapted the confident manner of those who were aware of their charm ... Noël Coward's influence spread even to the outposts of Rickmansworth and Poona ... All sorts of men suddenly wanted to look like Noël Coward - sleek ... clipped and well-groomed, with cigarette, a telephone, or cocktail in hand' (p. 154).
40. Noël Coward. *Not Yet the Dodo and Other Verses* (London: Heinemann, 1967), p. 34.
41. Maugham, *The Summing Up*, pp. 154-5.
42. *Ibid.*
43. Coward, *Play Parade Vol. 1*.
44. Coward, *Not Yet the Dodo and Other Verses*, p. 34.
45. Susan Sontag, *Against Interpretation* (London: Eyre and Spottiswoode, 1967), p. 288.
46. *The Times*, 26 January 1939.

47. New York *Times*, December 1969.
48. Coward, *Play Parade Vol. 1*, p. xvi.
49. Coward, *Present Indicative*, p. 158-9.
50. As quoted in Dick Richard (ed.), *The Wit of Noël Coward*, p. 58.
51. Coward, *Play Parade Vol. 1*, p. xvii
52. New York *Times*, 10 November 1957.
53. *Ibid.*
54. Coward, *Play Parade Vol. 5* (London: Heinemann, 1958), p. xxxii.
55. Ivor Brown, *Observer*, 29 January 1939.
56. Terence Rattigan, 'Noël Coward: An Appreciation of his work in the theatre', in Raymond Mander and Joe Mitchenson (eds), *Theatrical Companion to Coward* (London: Rockliff, 1957), p. 5.
57. *Ibid.*
58. As quoted in Castle, *Noël*, p. 139.
59. *Ibid.*

3: 'Savonarola in Evening Dress'?

1. Janet Flanner, *London Was Yesterday: 1934-1939* (London: Michael Joseph, 1975), p. 139.
2. Coward, *Future Indefinite*, p. 3.
3. New York *Times*, December 1969.
4. St. John Ervine in a lecture, 1932.
5. See A. J. P. Taylor; *English History: 1914-1945*, p. 260.
6. As quoted in Richards (ed.) *The Wit of Noël Coward*, p. 60.
7. Lustgarten, BBC-Radio, 1972.
8. 14 February 1932.
9. As quoted in Richards (ed.), *The Wit of Noël Coward*, p. 60.
10. Lustgarten, BBC-Radio, 1972.
11. James Agate, *Times*, 14 July 1931.
12. Lustgarten, BBC-Radio, 1972.
13. Coward, *Present Indicative*, p. 391.
14. *Ibid.*

15. Lesley, *The Life of Noël Coward*, p. 158.
16. *Ibid.*, p. 157.
17. As quoted in Mander and Mitchenson (eds.), *Theatre Companion to Coward*, p. 166.
18. A. J. P. Taylor, *English History: 1914–1945*, p. 298.
19. Coward, *Play Parade Vol. 1*, p. ix.
20. Coward, *Present Indicative*, p. 411.
21. *Ibid.*
22. *Ibid.*, p. 412.
23. 14 October 1931.
24. *Daily Mail*, 14 October 1931.
25. Ibid.
26. A. J. P. Taylor, *English History: 1914–1945*, p. 314.
27. Coward, *Present Indicative*, p. 412.
28. Coward, *Play Parade Vol. 1*, p. x.
29. Douglas Dunn, 'Pity the poor Philosophers: Coward's Comic Genius', *Encounter*, October 1980, p. 49.
30. Coward, *Present Indicative*, p. 131.
31. Noël Coward, 'Talking on Theatre', BBC-Radio, 19 September 1961.
32. Noël Coward, *Play Parade Vol. 4* (London: Heinemann, 1954), p. xiv.
33. Dunn, *Encounter*, October 1980, p. 51.
34. As quoted in Robert Rhodes James (ed.), *Chips: The Diaries of Sir Henry Chips Channon*, p. 176.
35. As quoted in Lesley, *The Life of Noël Coward*, p. 242.
36. Coward, 'London', Topical Talk–BBC Radio, 19 July 1940.
37. Morley, *A Talent to Amuse*, p. 212.
38. Coward, *The Lyrics of Noël Coward* (New York: Overlook Press, 1973), p. 205.
39. Ibid.
40. Morley, *A Talent to Amuse*, p. 212.
41. Coward, *Future Indefinite*, p. 113.
42. As quoted in Morley, *A Talent to Amuse*, p. 228.
43. *Ibid.*, p. 229.
44. As quoted in Mander and Mitchenson (eds.), *Theatrical Companion to Coward*, p. 355.

45. *Ibid.*, p. 356.

4: Ghosts in the Fun Machine

1. Keith Thomas, *Religion and the Decline of Magic* (London: Penguin Books, 1973), p. 717.
2. *Ibid.*, p. 717.
3. Hunter Davies, New York *Times*, December 1969.
4. As quoted in Lesley, *The Life of Noël Coward*, p. 247.
5. Coward, *Not Yet the Dodo and Other Verses*, p. 33.
6. As quoted in Richard Buckle (ed.), *Self-Portrait with Friends:* The Selected Diaries of Cecil Beaton (London: Weidenfeld and Nicolson, 1979), p. 91.
7. Graham Payn and Sheridan Morley (eds.), *The Noël Coward Diaries* (London: Weidenfeld and Nicolson, 1982). 11 May 1941.
8. *Ibid.*
9. *Ibid.*, 22 April 1941.
10. Coward, *Play Parade Vol. 5*, p. xxxii
11. Payn and Morley (eds), *The Noël Coward Diaries*, 10 May 1941.
12. Thomas, *Religion and the Decline of Magic*, p. 723.
13. Eric Bentley, 'Farce' in *The Life of the Drama* (New York: Atheneum, 1964), pp. 219–56.
14. Payn and Morley (eds.), *The Noël Coward Diaries*, 22 April 1941.
15. Coward, 'London', BBC-Radio, 19 July 1940.
16. Michael Goldman, *The Actor's Freedom* (New York: Viking, 1975). p. 154.
17. At 41, Wilde was one of the older writers of a comic masterpiece (*The Importance of Being Ernest*). Orton wrote *What the Butler Saw* at 34; Congreve was 30 when he wrote *Way of the World*; and Sheridan wrote *The Rivals* when he was 23 and *School for Scandal* at 26.
18. Coward, *Play Parade Vol. 6* (London: Heinemann, 1962), p. xiii.
19. New York *Times*, 10 November 1957.

5: Parting Shots

1. Tynan, *Curtains*, p. 128.
2. George Devine, the founder of the English Stage Company, was as early as 1943 comparing Coward to 'a well-paid chorus girl'. See Irving Wardle, *The Theatres of George Devine* (London: Jonathan Cape, 1978.), p. 91.
3. Tynan, *Curtains*, p. 86.
4. Coward, *Play Parade Vol. 5*, p. xvii.
5. Coward, 'My Very Loyal Public', *Daily Mail*, 13 May 1960.
6. Payn and Morley (eds.), *The Noël Coward Diaries*. On 14 November 1963, Coward's diary records his disaffection with his times this way: 'Our history, except for stupid, squalid social scandals, is over now. I despise the young, who see no quality in our great past and who spit, with phony, Left Wing disdain on all that we, as a race, have contributed to the living world.'
7. *Ibid.*, 11 September 1960.
8. *Ibid.*, 6 August 1960.
9. *Ibid.*, 2 May 1960.
10. *Ibid.*, 9 October 1960.
11. *Ibid.*, 9 October 1960.
12. *Ibid.*, 9 October 1960.
13. Although increasingly, his income came from cabaret and film roles, Coward's plays did better than limp along. *Pacific 1860* (1946), *Peace in Our Time* (1947), *South Sea Bubble* (1950), *Relative Values* (1951) and *Quadrille* (1952) are well below literary par but managed to run respectively for 129, 167, 276, 477, and 329 performances.
14. *Daily Mail*, 9 September 1960.
15. New York *Times*, 10 November 1957.
16. New York *Times*, December 1969.
17. Coward, *Play Parade Vol. 5*, p. xviii.
18. Coward, 'The Old Fashioned Revolutionaries', *Sunday Times*, 15 January 1961.

19. Coward, 'The Scratch and Mumble School', *Sunday Times*, 22 January 1961.
20. *Ibid.*
21. *Harper's Bazaar*, August 1960.
22. *Ibid.*
23. Kenneth Tynan, *Tynan Right and Left* (London: Longmans, 1967) p. 87.
24. Coward, *Play Parade Vol. 5*, p. xix.
25. Coward, *Sunday Times*, 22 January 1961.
26. *Ibid.*
27. Coward, *Play Parade Vol. 6*, p. 425.
28. Payn and Morley (eds.), *The Noel Coward Diaries*, 1 January 1961.
29. *Ibid.*, 22 April 1960.
30. As quoted in Lesley, *The Life of Noël Coward*, p. 458.
31. Payn and Morley (eds.), *The Noël Coward Diaries*.
32. Hunter Davies, New York *Times*, December 1969.
33. Coward, *Play Parade Vol. 5*, p. xvii.
34. Coward, *Sunday Times*, 15 January 1961.
35. Coward, *Play Parade Vol. 6*, p. xvii.
36. Coward, *Sunday Times*, 15 January 1961.
37. Payn and Morley (eds.), *The Noël Coward Diaries*, 11 September 1960.
38. *Ibid.*
39. As quoted in *Daily Mail*, 16 February 1982.
40. *Daily Mail*, 9 September 1960.
41. As quoted in Morley, *A Talent to Amuse*, p. 294.
42. *Ibid.*, p. 299.
43. Payn and Morley (eds.), *The Noël Coward Diaries*, 9 October 1960.
44. *Ibid*, 10 November 1960.
45. Hunter Davies, New York *Times*, December 1969.
46. As quoted in John Elsom, *British Post-War Theatre Criticism* (Routledge and Kegan Paul, 1981), p. 182.
47. *Ibid.*
48. *Ibid.*
49. As quoted in Lesley, *The Life of Noël Coward*, p. 505.

50. *Ibid.*, p. 507.
51. Tynan, *Curtains*, p. 60.
52. *Ibid.*, p. 60.
53. *Ibid.*, p. 59.
54. Payn and Morley (eds.), *The Noël Coward Diaries*.
55. As quoted in Lesley, *The Life of Noël Coward*, p. 507.
56. Epigram to Lesley, *The Life of Noël Coward*.
57. *Harper's Bazaar*, August 1960.

Bibliography

BOOKS BY NOËL COWARD

1. *Play Parade* (with Introductions by the author)
   Vol. 1 (Heinemann, 1934): *Cavalcade, Design for Living, Bitter-Sweet, Private Lives, Hay Fever, The Vortex, Post Mortem.*
   Vol. 2 (Heinemann, 1939): *This Year of Grace, Words and Music, Operette, Conversation Piece, Easy Virtue, Fallen Angels.*
   Vol. 3 (Heinemann, 1950): *The Queen Was in the Parlour, I'll Never Leave You, Sirocco, The Young Idea, The Rat Trap, This Was a Man, Home Chat, The Marquise.*
   Vol. 4 (Heinemann, 1954): *We Were Dancing, The Astonished Heart, 'Red Peppers', Hands Across the Sea, Fumed Oak, Shadow Play, Ways and Means, Still Life, Family Album, Present Laughter, This Happy Breed.*
   Vol. 5 (Heinemann, 1958): *Blithe Spirit, Peace in Our Time, Quadrille, Relative Values, Pacific 1860.*
   Vol. 6 (Heinemann, 1962): *Point Valaine, Ace of Clubs, South Sea Bubble, Nude with Violin, Waiting in the Wings.*
2. *Coward Plays* (Eyre Methuen Master Playwrights, 1979; distributed in USA by Grove Press, New York; introduced by Raymond Mander and Joe Mitchenson):
   Plays: One – Hay Fever, The Vortex, Fallen Angels, Easy Virtue.
   Plays: Two – Private Lives, Bitter-Sweet, The Marquise, Post-Mortem.
   Plays: Three – Design for Living, Cavalcade, Conversation Piece, To-night at 8:30 (I): Hands Across the Sea, Still Life, Fumed Oak.

175

Plays: Four - Blithe Spirit, Present Laughter, This Happy Breed, To-night at 8:30 (II): Ways and Means, The Astonished Heart, 'Red Peppers'.
Plays: Five - Relative Values, Waiting in the Wings, Look After Lulu, Suite in Three Keys.

3. *Suite in Three Keys* (Heinemann, 1966): *A Song at Twilight, Shadows of the Evening, Come into the Garden Maud.*

4. *Present Indicative* (London: Heinemann; New York: Doubleday, 1937).

5. *Future Indefinite* (London: Heinemann; New York: Doubleday, 1954).

6. *The Lyrics of Noël Coward* (London: Heinemann, 1965: New York: Doubleday).

7. *Not Yet the Dodo and Other Verses* (London: Heinemann, 1967).

8. *The Noël Coward Diaries*, edited by Graham Payn and Sheridan Morley (London: Weidenfeld and Nicolson, 1982; Boston: Atlantic-Little Brown, 1982).

BOOKS ABOUT NOËL COWARD

1. Charles Castle, *Noël* (London: W. H. Allen, 1972).

2. Cole Lesley, *The Life of Noël Coward* (London: Jonathan Cape 1976). Published in USA as *Remembered Laughter* (New York: Alfred A. Knopf, 1976).

3. Raymond Mander and Joe Mitchenson, *Theatrical Companion to Coward* (London: Rockliff, 1957; New York: Macmillan, 1957).

4. Sheridan Morley, *A Talent to Amuse* (London: Heinemann, 1969; New York: Doubleday, 1969).

5. Cole Lesley, Graham Payn and Sheridan Morley (eds.), *Noël Coward and His Friends* (London: Weidenfeld and Nicolson, 1979; New York: Doubleday, 1979).

Index